BRIAN JOHNSTON

Great Truths of the Gospel .... And the Errors People Often Make About It

HAYES
PRESS Christian Publisher

Contents

I

GREAT TRUTHS OF THE GOSPEL ...

1

ITS NEED

Have you ever stopped yourself from buying something by asking yourself: 'Do I really need this?' It's the great trick advertisers use to convince us that life would be unbearable without whatever it is they're promoting. Most of the time that's just an illusion created by the image-makers.

But over the next few studies, I'd like to share with you something that we all really do need. How can I know that when I don't even know you personally? Because we'll be talking about God's special offer to each one of us as described in the Bible. And because it's God who's making the offer we can be sure it's something we really do all need, something we simply can't afford to be without.

What we're talking about is what the Bible calls 'the Gospel'. The word means 'good news'. In this set of studies we hope to find out just why the Gospel is good news. But, as we say, the first step is to convince ourselves that it's something we really do need. There's a verse in the Bible which says: "*For we ourselves were also once foolish, disobedient, deceived, serving various lusts and pleasures, living in malice and envy, hateful and hating one another.*" That's what the apostle Paul wrote to someone called Titus. It's found in the letter in our Bibles called after Titus, and in chapter 3 verse 3 we have the words already quoted: "*For we ourselves were also once foolish, disobedient, deceived, serving various lusts and pleasures, living in malice and envy, hateful and hating one another.*" That's a description of what these early Christians were before they became believers on the Lord Jesus. And it's pretty powerful evidence for why we need the Gospel, isn't it? Disobedient and deceived; lusts and pleasures; malice and envy; hateful and hating - those four couplets show the full extent of our human depravity. That's why we need the Gospel for that's how God sees each and every one of us. No-one can go to heaven like that.

Let's just focus on the last of those four couplets. You remember the one? - it described us as hateful and hating. And how we react to one another is a reflection of our attitude to God himself. Maybe you think that's going a bit too far. Not that many people would describe themselves as militant atheists, and yet, according to the Bible, even the most ardent unconverted church-goer – even if he or she is an acclaimed as a pillar of society - is basically at enmity with God. Biblically, we're spoken of as being enemies in our minds by Paul in Colossians chapter 1. You can do all the right things and say all the right things and yet, without knowing Jesus Christ as your personal Saviour, your heart is hostile towards God, whether you suspect it or not. That's why the Gospel appeal can be summed up in words lifted from the end of Second Corinthians chapter 5 – and the words are: *"Be reconciled to God"*.

In January 1998, the then British Prime Minister, Tony Blair, paid an official visit to Japan. During his visit the Japanese made an official apology for their treatment of British prisoners of war during the Second World War. This extended to a package of measures which were offered so as to bring about reconciliation. Ill-treatment had alienated the men concerned and their families and made them hostile and so it was they, the British, who needed to be reconciled to the Japanese and not vice versa.

This reminds me of how the word is used in the Bible. God is never spoken of as needing to be reconciled to us. For - far from hating us - he already loves us. He hates our sin - that's true - but quite another matter. The hatred, the hostility, is all on our part. And yet Romans chapter 5 says: *"While we were still sinners, Christ died for us ... when we were enemies we were reconciled to God through the death of His Son."*

The story is told of Joe and Bill. In the past they'd been good friends but some offence had been caused which had resulted in a bitter feud between them. For years it'd gone on and now Joe was on his death-bed. He sent for Bill and explained he was afraid to enter eternity with things standing the way they were between the two of them. He told Bill he'd forgive all the insults hurled at him if Bill would forgive the things he'd said and done to him. Bill agreed and things were all settled. Eventually Bill stood up to go. He got to the door before Joe called: 'but remember it's all off if I recover!'

5

God's offer to us is not 'yes' and 'no' because a death has taken place to bring about reconciliation: the death of Jesus Christ, God's Son. Read again the words of Romans chapter 5 verse 10: *"when we were enemies we were reconciled to God through the death of His Son."* When by God's grace we believe that Jesus' death on the cross was for us, a tremendous change takes place in our nature and in our life.

There is a hymn which says, 'What a wonderful change in my life has been wrought since Jesus came into my heart' - the change we're talking about lies at the heart of what reconciliation means. Long ago, the word was used for the exchange of coins. It came to mean a change, any change. In the way the Bible uses it, it means in particular a change in our disposition from enmity to friendship towards God. Notice how the Bible describes the change:

"Therefore, if anyone is in Christ, he is a new creation; old things have passed away; behold, all things have become new. Now all things are of God, who has reconciled us to Himself through Jesus Christ, and has given us the ministry of reconciliation, that is, that God was in Christ reconciling the world to Himself, not imputing their trespasses to them, and has committed to us the word of reconciliation. Now then, we are ambassadors for Christ, as though God were pleading through us: we implore you on Christ's behalf, be reconciled to God."

God was in Christ reconciling the world to himself. What a lot is contained in these words! 'God was in Christ' takes us right back to the Christmas story of God's son coming to earth, being born into humanity for a special purpose - to die to obtain forgiveness for all who believe on him. That's what's meant by: *"God ... in*

Christ reconciling the world to Himself." That took place at the cross outside Jerusalem about 2000 years ago when God's son, as the man Jesus Christ, took our blame and place. We, the world, were at war with God, and while we were enemies Christ died for us.

There's a story from the Korean war where a South Korean Christian was captured by the communists. The communist officer in charge was ready to execute him by firing squad when he found out that he used to run an orphanage. For some twisted reason he now decided to spare the man but only so that he could watch his 19 year old son being shot in his place. When the war was over, that particular communist officer was tried by a war crimes tribunal and sentenced to death for such atrocities. Amazingly, the Christian whose son he'd shot came forward as sentence was being passed and pleaded emotionally for the officer's life to be spared. Because of the special circumstances, the request was granted. And later the communist officer received Christ and himself became a preacher of the Gospel.

It's a remarkable story of a Christian so full of the Spirit that he was able to forgive the man who'd shot his young son in cold blood. The man whose son he'd slain was pleading for him! Even that is overshadowed by the reality of what God has done in the giving of his son to die for all our wrongs and offences on the cross. And now, the God whose son we've slain - for our sins as we've thought put Him on the cross - the God whose son we've slain is pleading for us - pleading for us to be reconciled to him. Isn't that even more wonderful?! 'Be reconciled to God' is the appeal that sums up what our response to the God who gave his son for us must be. Perhaps, we could paraphrase it as:

7

'Get reconciled to God' - and do it now!

In conclusion, let's come back to the point we were making in defining the Gospel as to our need of it. We need the Gospel because we're enemies in our minds and wicked works against God. And as Titus 3 verse 3 explains this shows up in our relations amongst ourselves in disobedience and deceit; in lusts and pleasures; in malice and envy; and in being hateful and hating. What a description of our lost and needy state before a holy God!

The Bible here gives us real insight into God's view of us: as lacking in sense and sensibility; as Satan's dupes doing his pleasure; as wishing people ill and being jealous of their welfare; and capable of reciprocating hatred. Four ugly sets of twins I'm sure you'll agree. Together they plumb the depths of our fallen nature, our depravity before God. They alert us clearly to our need. But praise God as we'll see - if you carry on reading- the Gospel of his grace is exactly what we need!

2

ITS SOURCE

I n 1866 the Scottish explorer, medical doctor and missionary, David Livingstone, led an expedition to find the source
of the Nile, arguably the longest river in the world. Its main
source is Lake Victoria in east central Africa. (The so-called Blue
Nile begins in Ethiopia and is joined by the so-called White Nile
in Sudan before finally emerging into the Mediterranean.) Well,
little was heard from Livingstone for a while during this period.
Such was the concern of the international community that they
sent a journalist, Henry Morton Stanley, to find him. He did,
greeting him with the now famous words: 'Dr. Livingstone,
I presume?' Later, Livingstone continued his search for the
source of the Nile, eventually dying in what is now modern
Zambia in 1873.

Identifying the source of something is important. I'd like you
to examine with me the source of the Gospel of God. In this
series of studies, we're taking a look at the Christian Gospel, the
good news message offered through the Bible to each and every
one of us. All the points that define what we're talking about

are to be found in Paul's writing to someone called Titus. This letter is found near to the back of our Bibles. We're studying its third chapter and verses 3 to 8. These verses form such a complete summary of the Christian message – conveyed in so few words - that some scholars have suggested that they may be based on what was an early Christian creed. Whether that hunch is correct or not doesn't really matter since these verses are included within the Bible - and that's what does really matter.

Previously, we began by considering verse 3 and we saw from there the four ugly twins of disobedience and deceit; lusts and pleasures; malice and envy; and hateful and hating. We saw that together these present to us - very clearly - our need for the Gospel. Now from verse 4, I'd like us to identify the source of this much needed Gospel. That's what we find in verse 4: *"But when the kindness and the love of God our Saviour toward man appeared."* What a change from the previous verse with all those ugly twins! - those things which show us the extent of our need before God. We certainly can't expect to find the source of salvation within ourselves, given that our nature is as corrupted as verse 3 has made out. That's why the New Age philosophy – and, in fact, all self-help systems promising salvation by our own works – they're hopelessly and totally wrong - we cannot save ourselves. Instead we're in need of help which originates outside of ourselves.

Immediately after the text describing our depraved condition, we read *"But when the kindness and the love of God our Saviour toward man appeared."* This is one of some great Bible verses that begin with the word 'but.' There's another similar one I came across the other day in my reading. It's in Paul's letter to the Ephesians chapter 2. Again, he's been talking there about things like disobedience and lusts. Then he turns to his fellow Christians and says: *"we ... were ... just as the others. But God ..."* There's the 'but.' *'But God, who is rich in mercy, because of His great love with which He loved us, even when we were dead in trespasses, made us alive.'*

In Ephesians, as in Titus, the talk is first of our need followed by the source of deliverance. And the source of this good news is to be found in the kindness and love of God. The source of hope and salvation doesn't lie within the scope of human self-improvement, but in divine kindness and love. If you've experienced God's love, you may want to sing the hymn that says 'God's love to us will never cease, unlimited it flows.' Even the mighty Nile, the world's longest river, that we were thinking about earlier can't compare with the unceasing flow of God's love. It seems to me that the writer of that wonderful hymn felt overwhelmed by it.

Like the little lad on the ship who asked his dad how big God's love was. Children have the knack of asking the most unanswerable questions sometimes, don't they? Father and son stood in silence for a few moments on the deck of the great liner out on the ocean. Then dad turned to the little boy and said: 'Do you see away over there?' He pointed eastwards away to the horizon. Then he turned him round to face the south. 'Do you see away over there?' he asked. Again, the boy nodded. His father pointed him to all the compass points in turn. In every direction all that could be seen was the vast expanse of ocean stretching out to the horizon. 'Do you see all that', Dad said finally, 'well God's love is bigger than that!' 'Wow', the boy

said, 'do you realize, Dad - we're right in the middle of it all!'
How true. How true of the love that God has lavished upon us,
commending it to us in that while we were still sinners his son,
Jesus Christ died, for us.

Now coming back to Titus and verse 4, where, you remember,
it speaks of the kindness and love of God having 'appeared.'
Sometimes the Bible puts an awful lot in a very few words - even
in one single word. Here's a case in point. The word 'appeared'
we've just read actually embraces the birth, death, life and
resurrection of the Lord Jesus. The same word is found a few
verses earlier in the second chapter when Paul writes: "*For the
grace of God that brings salvation has appeared to all men.*" That's
verse 11 and in verse 13 he goes on to say: "*looking for the blessed
hope and glorious appearing of our great God and Saviour Jesus
Christ who gave Himself for us.*" Did you notice the repetitions of
'appeared' and 'appearing'? If you've ever come across the word
'epiphany' - most likely in a church connection - then that is in
fact the original word behind the mention of these 'appearings'.
When verse 11 talks about the saving grace of God appearing, we
could perhaps call that 'the epiphany of grace.' That was the
grace of God seen in Jesus Christ.

The basic sense of this word 'epiphany' is to shine. Into a world
darkened by sin, God sent his son, Jesus. The prophets long ago
had foretold of the coming of a great light. Just before we come
to the popular Christmas verse, Isaiah 9 and 6: "*For unto us a
Child is born, unto us a Son is given; and the government will be upon
His shoulder. And His name will be called Wonderful, Counselor,
Mighty God, Everlasting Father, Prince of Peace*" - just before that
verse, we read in verse 2 of the same 9th chapter of Isaiah that:

"the people who walked in darkness have seen a great light; those who dwelt in the land of the shadow of death, upon them a light has shined." In other words, with the coming of Christ, the true light entered the world in the epiphany of God's grace.

But then, back in Titus, we read also about *"the blessed hope and glorious appearing of our great God and Saviour Jesus Christ."* If what we read of in verse 11 was the epiphany of God's grace, then this must be the epiphany of God's glory. God's glory will be seen at the time of the Second Advent - the time of the return of Jesus Christ. You know how on town street maps there's usually a big red or blue arrow with the words 'you are here.' When I read in this Titus letter about the epiphany of grace and the epiphany of glory, I'm reminded of one of these direction finders. I can almost visualize a big arrow in God's Word pointing between the two epiphanies which are the two Advents of Christ. Pointing between them, and saying to us today: 'you are here' - living between these two marvellous appearings of the Son of God! The first took place almost 2,000 years ago; the second is yet to take place - perhaps at any time. And for the believer in Christ it will be a blessed and a glorious experience!

What, then, have we learned about the Gospel so far from Titus chapter 3? Previously, from verse 3, we discovered 'its need,' in other words, our need of the Gospel because of the fact that the human nature of each and every one of us is corrupted by sin. And from verse 4, we've been exploring 'its source': and we've been tracing the source of the Gospel back to the kindness and love of God - God's kindness which he shows even to the ungrateful. That's the greatest discovery that anyone can ever make: to discover that God loves them.

3

ITS GROUND

I'd now like to consider with you the ground of the Gospel – in other words, the basis on which the Gospel rests. Or to put it more directly: is the basis for our salvation what we do or what God has done? Let me begin by saying that I'm a great believer in Do-It-Yourself whether its conveyancing or tax assessment or car maintenance or tinkering with a computer - I like having a go. There's a sense of achievement in succeeding after a bit of a struggle. But when it comes to the most important decision of our lives, when it comes to the issue of our salvation, the Bible, God's Word, has taught me that there's absolutely no way that I can do it myself as far as getting to heaven is concerned. Psalm 49 tells us that the salvation of the soul is costly and must be left alone for ever.

But there's a popular rumour going around - actually it's a total lie and it was started a long time ago - a rumour that says that in this matter of securing God's favour and gaining a place in heaven you can also do that yourself. Maybe you've heard some versions of this rumour, like: 'unlock your potential by discovering the 'god' within you'; or 'so long as you're sincere it doesn't matter which religion you subscribe to'; or 'simply do the best you can and God, if he's there, well, he's bound to approve of that.'

Many religious groups or cults stress what they say you have to do in order to be sure of our future. Very often this involves carrying out the instructions of some influential personality who's leading the group, or spreading the group's message to get new recruits, or learning how to support what's being taught in the publications produced by them. But can any of these things save us? Millions of people all over the world hope they can. But, can they truly save us? The answer the Bible gives is an emphatic 'no'! To show that, in a moment, we're going to read from Paul's letter to Titus chapter 3 verse 5. But first let me remind you that earlier in this series - our series on defining the Gospel, or the good news God has for us - we've already considered its need and its source from the two previous verses.

Having that background in mind, we're talking now about the ground of the Gospel, in other words, the basis on which we can be saved. Let's now listen to verse 5. By the way, when we speak about 'being saved' we are, of course, talking about being saved from the punishment our sins deserve. Let's now go to Titus 3 verse 5: *"Not by works of righteousness which we have done, but according to His mercy He saved us, through the washing of regeneration and renewing of the Holy Spirit."* It really couldn't be clearer, could it? We don't - we can't - save ourselves. *"He saved us"* is what this Bible verse says - and that's God - God saves us. And God doesn't save us by simply taking note of the good things we do in life. It's 'not by works of righteousness which we have done.' In other words, it's not a matter of making a pilgrimage to some place regarded as being holy; nor is it about performing noble acts to impress God and others; the issue isn't whether you've had a lifelong, faithful commitment to a particular church or religious institution or simply lived a decent life.

It's true that some lives are more moral or good than others, at least as far as we can judge them. Some people will do anyone a good turn; others couldn't care less, they're only interested in themselves. I want you to imagine two people: one living a very respectable, charitable, church-going life; and the other a shifty good-for-nothing type – a bit of a petty criminal perhaps. Well, surely there's a difference between them. Of course, there is. I guess we could imagine it by thinking of the 'good' person standing on the top of a mountain and the 'bad' person way down below almost at sea-level. Such a difference between the two if we're thinking of their height above sea-level! But neither one of them can touch the stars. The stars are hopelessly out of reach whether you're on a mountain or in a valley. And it's like that with God's standards. No matter how much better we believe we are than anyone else, when judged by God's perfect standards, we all fall hopelessly far short. His standard is unreachable.

The Bible itself uses another illustration - one that's based on the idea of dressing up. Instead of it being the difference between standing at the top or bottom of a mountain; it's the idea of different standards of dress, say between a tramp and someone dressed in their Sunday best. But what's God's verdict? Through the prophet Isaiah, God says in chapter 64 verse 6:

that *"All our righteousnesses are like filthy rags."* This shows us that even when we make a real effort to keep up appearances, even when our good deeds and general helpfulness draws the admiration and respect of others, God's not impressed. Even if we live constantly at the 'Sunday-best' level, nearly always mannerly and kind, God still says: *"All our righteousnesses are like filthy rags."*

Paul, when he was writing the Bible letter to the Romans, was comparing himself and religious people with others and asked the usual question: *"Are we better than they?"* (Romans 3:9). Then he answered his own question by quoting from an earlier part of the Bible - what it says may seem surprising - but it agrees with what we're saying: *"There is none who does good, no, not one ... all have sinned and fall short of the glory of God"* (Romans 3:12,23). Here we have it again: while we may be tempted to say that some are good and better than others, what God's Word says is that as far as getting to heaven is concerned, as far as being acceptable to God is concerned, on our own we all fall short, no one is good enough.

Well, you might say, I thought you said the Gospel is good news. It is, but to see how, we need to read further in our verse from Titus. *"Not by works of righteousness which we have done, but according to His mercy He saved us, through the washing of regeneration and renewing of the Holy Spirit."* It's according to his mercy that God saves people. What none of us can do, God is prepared to do himself because he's merciful. To show mercy to someone is not to let them suffer the fate that they well and truly deserve.

17

The story is told of a woman appealing to Napoleon for the life of her son. Napoleon replied that it was the young man's second offence and justice demanded that he should be punished. 'I'm not demanding justice', his mother responded, 'I'm begging for mercy!' 'Mercy?' Napoleon cried, 'He doesn't deserve mercy!' To this the mother replied: 'Sir, it would not be mercy if it was deserved. Please be merciful.' At this Napoleon agreed to show mercy.

God showed mercy at the cross. This is the ground of the Gospel. God invites us to take our stand on his mercy. Maybe, before, you were inclined to take your stand on your own righteousness, believing your life of good deeds made you to be deserving of heaven. I hope you see now from God's Word in Titus that that's impossible. It's not by works of righteousness which we do. But it's by God's mercy that he saves us. We simply don't deserve salvation. Justice, the justice of God, demands that our sins be punished. Our unkind and unclean thoughts; our rash and bitter words; our careless actions and even those times when we simply didn't do something that we knew was the right thing to do - all this deserves judgement from a holy God. But by nature, he's also merciful. He showed that when he gave his Son to die 'for our sins' as the Bible says.

There's just space to mention what happens when we do take our stand on God's mercy, believing his son died for us. Our studied text tells us about that too. Shall we read it once again? "*Not by works of righteousness which we have done, but according to His mercy He saved us, through the washing of regeneration and renewing of the Holy Spirit.*" Regeneration basically means to be born-again. It was the Lord Jesus himself who first said to a high church-goer of his day: 'You must be born again'. We hear mention of such-a-body being a 'born again Christian', but what does it really mean? It refers to someone who receives Jesus Christ as their personal Saviour through faith. To such a person God gives a new start, a new nature and a new life. It's been said that if you're born once you'll die twice - for missing out on heaven is called the second death in the Bible: being separate from God for ever. But if you're born twice, you'll only ever die once. The most you may know is physical death, but then you'll go to be with your saviour. This regeneration is worth knowing, isn't it?

And what was that about 'renewing of the Spirit' at the end of our verse? Well, to all who give their heart to him, God gives his Holy Spirit to come and live there. A constant companion; with divine help and strength for all the problems of life. You don't have to wait till heaven; the blessings start now the moment you believe!

4

ITS MEANS

There are many occasions when it's helpful to define the terms of a proposed deal, or perhaps simply ask someone: 'exactly what did you mean by that?' – especially if they appear to be using a word in an ambiguous way or else are using a word that's not commonly understood. An example of the second example might be the word 'Gospel.' It simply means God's good news, but what is that? God is offering forgiveness, but how and to whom? These are some of the issues we're dealing with in this series of studies which essentially focus on defining the Gospel.

We've already thought about **the need** for the Gospel, as we considered some of the effects of our sinful nature from Titus chapter 3. Then we discovered that **the source** of the Gospel lay in God's own love and kindness towards us. That was verse 4 of the same chapter. When we then asked about **the basis** of God's salvation – his forgiveness of sinners – the Bible taught us from verse 5 that the ground of the Gospel was God's own mercy and certainly not our righteousness.

Now we come to the second half of the same verse in Titus chapter 3 that we were looking at before - the 5th verse - where it says: "*He* [God] *saved us, through the washing of regeneration and renewing of the Holy Spirit.*" This brings us now to the point of how the change the Gospel brings actually takes effect in our lives. In other words, we're considering 'its means' or mechanism - or how it is that the Gospel comes to us. The means of salvation is - according to our text - regeneration and renewing. But what are they?

Regeneration basically means to be born-again. It was the Lord Jesus himself who first said to a high church-goer of his day: "You must be born again." And today we hear mention of such-a-body being a 'born again Christian', but what does it really mean to be a born-again Christian? It refers to someone who's received Jesus Christ as their personal saviour through faith. To such a person, God gives a new start, a new nature and a new life. It's been said that if you're born once you'll die twice - for missing out on heaven is called the second death in the Bible: being separate from God for ever. But if you're born twice, you'll only ever die once. The most you may know is physical death, but then you'll go to be with your Saviour. I'd say that this regeneration is worth knowing, wouldn't you?

As we've said it was to one of the religious leaders of that time - someone who might have been regarded as having been in favour with God because of his religious and moral life - that Jesus said that he must be *"born anew ... born of water and the Spirit ... born of the Spirit."* This command in John 3:3-8 indicates the first of 3 things vital to this new birth experience. It's something which is said to be 'of the Holy Spirit.' In other words, it's a change

21

brought about within us by the working of God the Holy Spirit. As well as the work of the Holy Spirit being required to bring about this event, the apostle Peter speaks of it being *"through the word of God"* in First Peter 1:23, where he addresses his readers as those who had been born again by means of *"the incorruptible seed"* of the Word of God. When we receive God's Word as sinners, acknowledging its testimony concerning ourselves and Christ as being the truth, then we are born again as a result.

And thirdly, John, in opening his gospel, makes it plain that this wonderful event takes place when we receive Jesus Christ, God's Son, as our personal Saviour. He writes *"as many as received him ... become children of God,"* and he goes on to emphasise that all who *"believe on his name"* are born of God. How wonderful to think that by receiving Christ by faith we are brought into this relationship with God which can never cease to exist, since obviously a birth, whether natural or spiritual, is an irreversible process. In other words, it's a work of the Divine Spirit, and God's Word is instrumental in bringing it about, and we, too, have our part to play – but only through exercising faith.

The famous preacher, Spurgeon, once told the story of a native American (or 'First Nations' person) who wanted so much to become English that he even changed his style of dress, his name, and learned to speak English, before the truth dawned that it was all to no avail, for how could he become English without having been born English! Spurgeon used that story to illustrate how many in his day, and still today, try to change their behaviour, and take the name of Christians, and even learn to speak the religious language of prayer and the hymnbook in an equally futile attempt to get right with God as a result of these efforts of theirs. The point is, that in order to enter God's family and so be sure of going to heaven, we must be born again as a citizen of heaven.

Our new birth is also the beginning of a life, for we learn from John 5 verse 24 that from the moment we believe we have eternal life. And, just as the ordinary birth of a child is usually a source of great joy to all concerned, so the Lord Jesus taught that there is joy in heaven over one sinner who repents and enters God's family (Luke 15:10). Let me remind you that we're thinking about how the Gospel actually comes to us. The second part of Titus chapter 3 verse 5 sums it up in two words: one 'regeneration' which we've been thinking about; and the other 'renewing' which we'll come on to now. Remember the mention of the 'renewing of the Spirit' at the end of our verse? What is that? Well, to all who give their heart to him, God gives his Holy Spirit to come and live there. A constant companion; divine help and strength for all the problems of life. You don't have to wait till heaven; the blessings start now the moment you believe!

All who belong to Christ by saving faith, have, without exception, the Bible teaches, received the indwelling Spirit. It's not an option or even a later blessing for only a few. No, just as Christ is now physically absent from all believers here, so he has sent his Spirit to be in each and every believer. The Lord Jesus described the Holy Spirit as *"another Helper"* in John 14. The word 'helper' comes from a word meaning to draw alongside. Isn't that precious? Often, we struggle with troubling personal and spiritual concerns - in all these and at all times we have someone alongside us to help us. And that someone is God's Spirit. How gracious of him to make these poor hearts of ours his home! And he's always at hand just when we need him, he's always alongside - for he's permanently residing in our hearts.

Perhaps, sometimes we wish we'd been around when the Lord was here on earth. Wouldn't it have been marvellous to go around with him witnessing the miracles and listening to his sermons and prayers. But when the Lord promised us 'another' helper; the word 'another' means 'another of the very same kind.' All the eternal qualities of the Lord Jesus are, of course, shared by the Holy Spirit. And he's available or 'on call' for us 24 hours a day, 7 days a week. Surely, that's the main thing about what we're saying: by living in us, the Spirit of God is making himself and all the resources of God available to us at all times!

With such a holy Guest, we should remember not to grieve him - he's a person, not simply an influence as many wrongly teach - he's a person with emotions just as the Bible equally speaks of him having a 'mind' (Romans 8:27) and a 'will' (1 Corinthians 12:11). That's why Ephesians 4 verse 30 says: *"Do not grieve the Holy Spirit of God"* and mentions corrupt or unwholesome speech as an example of something that will grieve him. Since he indwells us, and our bodies are temples of the Holy Spirit, we're to glorify God with our bodies.

Let's ask ourselves: what have we learnt from this study in Titus in connection with how the Gospel comes to us? Our text from chapter 3 came from the end of verse 5 and says: *"He* [God] *saved us, through the washing of regeneration and renewing of the Holy Spirit."* From that we've seen that our sins are washed away when by faith we're born again by receiving the testimony of God's Word. And along with God's Word belongs God's Spirit who enables us to experience and live our new life.

5

ITS CENTRE

When your car won't start some morning and you call out assistance, what you really want is someone who can quickly diagnose the cause of the problem. Nothing can be put right until we find out what's wrong. What a relief when an expert goes right to the heart of the problem! Getting to the heart of something - that's what we plan to do in this particular study - to go right to the heart of the Gospel, the Christian message.

We've been looking at the third chapter of the Bible letter written by Paul to someone called Titus. It's here that the Apostle Paul summarizes the Gospel. I guess the first question to ask is why the need, what's wrong with us that we should need this Good News? Well, having begun at verse 3, we were certainly left in no doubt as to what's wrong! Our disobedience and deceit, our lusts and pleasures, our malice and envy, as well as our being hateful and hating were all paraded before us. I'm reminded of something the author and speaker, C.S. Lewis once said. He was a greatly respected university teacher, but when he looked deeply into his motives and private thoughts, he wrote: 'For the first time I examined myself with a seriously practical purpose. And there I found what appalled me: a zoo of lusts, a bedlam of ambitions, a nursery of fears, a harem of fondled hatreds. My name was legion.'

The Spirit of God convicts us all of sin. And when we call upon God for assistance, he goes right to the heart of the matter: telling us that we need a new nature. But how can this transformation take place? We're back to what we were thinking about in our last study, when from the end of verse 5 of Titus 3 we spoke about the new birth, or regeneration. When Jesus Christ himself was asked about how this new birth happens, he immediately went on to predict his death on the cross. And that's where we come to as we now arrive at verse 6 of this little section of our Bibles – this section of Titus where the Gospel is so fully yet so briefly defined. In verse 6 we read of the *Spirit "whom He* [God] *poured out on us abundantly through Jesus Christ our Saviour."*

Now that we've come almost to the middle of this section, the first mention of *"Jesus Christ our Saviour"* certainly brings us to the centre, or heart, of the Gospel message. The Lord Jesus himself proclaimed his centrality to the Christian message when he announced in John chapter fourteen verse 6: *"I am the way, the truth, and the life. No one comes to the Father except through Me."* That's remarkably exclusive teaching, and Jesus had by then become famous for his teaching, for his reported miracles, as well as for his conflicts with the religious authorities of the day. They felt threatened by his popularity and, eventually, succeeded in having him arrested and tried.

Pontius Pilate, the Roman governor, held Jesus to be innocent of the charges made by the religious leaders against Jesus. He wanted to release Jesus. But under pressure from the local crowds, he ordered death by crucifixion. He then attempted to distance himself from the decision by washing his hands in public. Jesus' body was laid to rest in the tomb of Joseph of Arithmathea, one of his more influential followers. Three days later, the Bible claims, he rose from the dead. It's definitely not possible to conclude from his life-story that this Jesus - also known to Roman and Jewish historians by the way - to conclude that this Jesus was only a good man or a fine teacher. His character was marked by humility and sanity and yet his claims, as we've already seen, were extraordinary to say the least. He claimed he could forgive sins. He said he'd rise from the dead and return in the time of the end to judge the world.

Open-minded, honest enquirers are really faced with a very stark choice indeed. Either we make of Jesus exactly what the jealous Jewish religious leaders did - that he was a fraudster and blasphemer - perhaps the greatest con-man who's ever lived - a view which goes against all the testimony of his life and the influence he's wielded down through the centuries - or we accept Jesus for who he himself claimed to be - the Son of God. As one Archbishop of Canterbury has put it: 'either we judge him as being terribly amiss, or we let him judge us'. The middle ground of him being just a good man, a good teacher is impossible, for good men don't tell lies, which Jesus did if he really isn't the Son of God.

Our focus now, then, is on this wonderfully unique Person whom the Bible declares to be God's son. Peter and John were among his first followers. For three years they lived together, worked together, wept together, ate together and shared a common purse. They walked hundreds of miles, got into tight corners, and grew tired together. They knew one another really well. It's truly remarkable, then, that Peter could apply this Old Testament statement to Jesus: *"He committed no sin, and no deceit was found in His mouth."* It's a sad fact of life that the better we get to know someone we really admire, the more we inevitably begin to see their insecurities, weaknesses, character flaws and blind-spots.

But, in contrast, and just as remarkable as Peter's testimony, we find John saying about Jesus that: *"In Him is no sin."* Jesus, they realized, had no personal sense of sin. This was the Jesus who allowed himself to be stripped and nails be driven through his hands and feet. The cross was then raised, and he was left hanging in the hot sun between two criminals. Soldiers gambled for his single worldly possession of any note: a seamless robe. Later, his side was pierced with a spear to make sure he was dead. While they were doing all this to him, Jesus cried out from the cross: *"Father, forgive them. They don't know what they are doing."*

What was going on? Surely, he didn't belong there. There's a story told about the Korean war featuring a hill known as Triangle hill. At one point, American forces were beaten back from the hill. Immediately, they regrouped and calling on all available support they set out to regain possession of this strategic location on the battlefield. They succeeded, but at some cost. Later a group of US marines noticed one of their number standing a little way off. When they went over, they found him stooped over the lifeless corpse of a US major. There were tears rolling down the young soldiers' cheeks. Sometimes the toughest of men cry. Motioning to the Major's body he said: 'He didn't have to be here. He volunteered. He could have been safely back at Headquarters with the other high-ranking officers. He didn't belong on this hill!'

Those words have stayed with me. 'He didn't belong on this hill'. No, but evidently he was there. The very same words apply in the fullest sense to the Lord Jesus Christ and the hill outside Jerusalem where he was executed. As we've thought together about the kind of person he was and life that he lived, surely it's obvious that he didn't belong on 'Skull hill.' He didn't deserve to be there. But he was there - for you and for me. The Bible devotes a great deal of space to the meaning of the cross. The cross reveals the depth of human sin. It was human pride that opposed Jesus. It was human greed which betrayed Him. It was human cruelty that had him impaled on that torture stake, reputably the cruellest form of execution ever devised by man.

We see among rulers and governments - at all levels internationally - the abuse of power. People take advantage of position and status to secure favours for themselves. They act as though they are a law to themselves, throwing their weight about, harassing staff, generally behaving as though they were accountable to no one. How often it's been demonstrated that power does indeed corrupt and absolute power corrupts absolutely. But - what a contrast - rather than using his power to dominate, Jesus chose to submit to the worst that people could do. The power of God is consistently seen in symbols of weakness - in a manger and on a cross. This is power restrained and directed by love. One of the most famous of Bible quotations begins: *"God so loved the world that He gave His only begotten Son ..."* (John 3:16).

When Jesus died, the land was covered in daytime darkness. It was as though the heavens themselves were saying: this is the blackest day of all in earth history. 'Look to Me', the Saviour invites. See him there: his back lacerated with the ferocious Roman scourging, a mass of torn flesh; his brow bloodied from where they pressed the thorny crown in; his face black and blue from the pummelling of the soldiers in the hours before; his hands and feet nailed to the cross; his mouth dry and intolerably thirsty; and the whole scene plunged into that God-forsaken blackness.

Tell me what you see? The Christ as merely depicted in relics and works of art, or the Son of God who loved you and gave himself up for you? Jesus' death on the cross was 'mission accomplished' as shown by the fact that three days later he rose from the dead and returned to heaven. Sounds incredible? But have you checked out the evidence for yourself? A former Lord Chief Justice of England was convinced and said: 'There exists such overwhelming evidence, positive and negative, factual and circumstantial, that no intelligent jury in the world could fail to bring in the verdict that the resurrection story is true.' This is the central issue of the Gospel. *"Believe on the Lord Jesus Christ and you will be saved"* (Acts 16:31). Believe in him and rejoice in knowing your sins all forgiven today.

6

ITS GOAL

I t's sad to see someone who doesn't have a goal in life. Perhaps an older person who's giving up in the battle against losing their faculties, finding it just too much effort to keep going; or what's possibly even sadder: seeing a young person leading an aimless existence and wrecking their body with addictive substances. All that God does is purposeful, and he's made us to be satisfied only with a purposeful existence. When Jesus Christ said: *"I am the way, the truth and the life"* (John 14:6), he was offering the possibility of the ultimate in direction and meaning in life to each one of us who come to know him as saviour and friend.

In coming now to the seventh Bible verse in Paul's letter to Titus chapter 3, I want us to consider what the goal of the Gospel is – what the goal of the Good News of God is. It's there in Titus 3 we also find the words: *"that having been justified by His grace we should become heirs according to the hope of eternal life."* As we now turn to think of the Gospel in terms of its goal, what we're doing is we're thinking about where the Gospel leads us to. This seems to be the main idea in the last part of the verse where we read about becoming heirs according to the hope of eternal life. But before we come to that, let's think a bit about the first part where it talks about being justified by his grace.

It's this idea of God's grace that more than anything else defines the Gospel of God. Long ago 'grace' was a word people used to mean a favour, an undeserved favour performed out of kindness. It was something quite beyond the call of duty done without expectation of anything in return, and was therefore commendable. But it was always something you did for a friend, never for an enemy. But when the New Testament was written, and in it this word was used, its meaning was lifted to an altogether higher plane. God's favour in connection with the Gospel is something he shows to those who are his enemies. For as Romans 5 verse 8 reminds us: *"God demonstrates His own love toward us, in that while we were still sinners, Christ died for us."*

As an illustration of this, let me share with you a story from the time of the American Revolutionary War. Among the people living in one Pennsylvanian town in those days were two men: one was a preacher of the Gospel, a church pastor called Peter; and the other whose name was Michael was a bit of a rogue. In fact, more than that he was a downright rascal. He took every opportunity he could find to make life difficult for the preacher: he made all sorts of false accusations against him. But then one day Michael found himself in court being tried before George Washington, seventy miles away in Philadelphia. The charge brought against him was treason and if found guilty he would be sentenced to death.

When pastor Peter heard of his plight, he set out to walk the seventy miles to the court in Philadelphia. As it happened, he was a friend - or at least an acquaintance - of General Washington. Maybe you think he was going to make sure he was once and for all rid of this troublesome character who made his life such a misery. But no, you'd be quite wrong. When he arrived in court, he actually appealed to Washington for Michael's life to be spared. Knowing nothing of the background, General Washington simply said that in this case he was unable to accept the appeal for clemency that Peter was making on behalf of his friend Michael. 'No, wait!', cried Peter, 'the accused is not my friend, far from it, for years he's been my bitterest critic and worst enemy!' General Washington was so impressed that someone should walk seventy miles in order to appeal to save the life of his enemy that he granted the pardon. Later, Michael and Peter walked home together - now as friends.

That's just a little illustration that appeals to me, as being an illustration of the far more wonderful thing that God has done in the giving of his son for those who at that time were still enemies to him. According to the Gospel, the great favour that God did for us through the giving of his son to die for us was to make it possible to justify us. What does that mean, you ask? Someone has helpfully noticed that the word 'justification' sounds a little like 'just-as-if' I'd never sinned. And that's exactly how God comes to view us when we receive his Good News message. He forgives all the sins of the man or woman who believes on the Lord Jesus, but more than that - so far-reaching was the effect of Christ's death - that God is able to view the once-guilty sinner as though they were righteous, never having sinned! He pronounces him or her as 'not guilty!'

And as Martin Luther discovered from the Bible letter to the Romans more than four centuries ago, this wonderful change takes place in our lives through faith. We are, the Bible teaches, justified by faith through God's grace. Can there be any better news than that? And yet with God there's always more! Titus 3 verse 7 tells us that we're justified by his grace so that we should become heirs according to the hope of eternal life. Now what does this mean? This sounds as though it has something to say to us about where the Gospel is leading us, but what exactly is it saying? First of all, let me make it clear what it's not saying. When it says 'hope of eternal life' don't think that the believer on the Lord Jesus has to wait until sometime in the future in order to receive the gift of eternal life. I'm afraid many people think that, but let's settle the issue with the words of the Lord Jesus in John's Gospel chapter 5 and verse 24: *"he who hears My word and believes in Him who sent Me has everlasting life, and shall not come into judgement, but has passed from death into life."*

Jesus speaks about the believer and the results of his faith in the past, present and future. When we believe on him, Christ promises three things: first is we have passed from death into life – please notice, that's already happened, we're no longer *"dead in our trespasses and sins"*; second, we actually have, now, the gift of eternal life, it begins at the new birth; and third, and this one is future, we will never stand before God to be judged for our sins – never ever!

The Christian believer is definitely not merely hoping that he or she will one day receive eternal life, for they already possess it. Let's notice carefully what our current text from Titus is really saying. It talks about us becoming heirs according to the hope of eternal life. In other words, this is mention of a future heavenly inheritance that will one day be ours in accordance with the full assurance of the eternal life we have now.

It's worth getting this absolutely straight: the Bible doesn't use the word 'hope' in the way we often do - meaning something on a wish list, that we may or may not have any chance of getting. No, 'hope' in the Bible sense means something certain, something absolutely assured because God has promised it, and his word is his bond, for it cannot be broken. The very fact that we already have eternal life is itself the guarantee of more blessings to come. Paul, in his writings in the Bible actually uses the word hope quite a lot. He doesn't only talk about the hope of eternal life (Titus 1:2;3:7), but also of the hope of salvation (1 Thessalonians 5:8), the hope of the Gospel (Colossians 1:23), the hope of righteousness (Galatians 5:5), the hope of our calling (Ephesians 4:4), the hope of the glory of God (Romans 5:2), and the hope and resurrection of the dead (Acts 23:6).

Probably all these expressions are aspects of what we might generally call 'the Gospel hope'. It's the heavenly inheritance which'll materialize at the return of the Lord Jesus Christ for all true believers. As Peter could say in his First letter chapter 1 verse 3: "*Blessed be the God and Father of our Lord Jesus Christ, who according to His abundant mercy has begotten us again to a living hope through the resurrection of Jesus Christ from the dead, to an inheritance incorruptible and undefiled and that does not fade away, reserved in heaven for you.*"

This is what the Gospel leads to. In a sense this is its goal. 'The sky not the grave is our goal' we sing in one of our great hymns and it's true. In contrast to the dead-end hopes of this world, hopes that end at death, the hope of the Christian believer is described as a living hope, one that outlives this life, one which is bound up with the world to come. It's a hope that's underpinned by the sure and well-known promise of the Lord Jesus in John 14 verse 2: *"In My Father's house are many mansions; if it were not so, I would have told you. I go to prepare a place for you."* The words *"if it were not so I would have told you"* have the ring of total assurance, spoken as they are by the truest of men: the son of God from heaven.

7

ITS EVIDENCE

With this chapter, we draw the first half of our studies to a close. We've been looking at the third chapter of Paul's letter to Titus. We started a few chapters ago at verse 3 and now we get to verse 8.

These verses we find in Titus chapter 3 are packed with explanations which describe God's Good News from many different angles. Together we've thought about **'its need'** on account of our sinfulness; then **'its source'** arising from the loving kindness of God himself; and after that **'its ground'** - that on which it rests being clearly stated to be God's mercy, not our good deeds; then from the second part of verse 5 we talked about **'its means'** when we saw the new birth is how it comes to us; next we focused on **'its centre'** in the person of Jesus Christ, the son of God who loved us and gave himself for us; and lastly from verse 7 we considered **'its goal'**, leading to a future heavenly inheritance; so to finish at verse 8, I want us to think about **'its evidence'** - how it proves itself as real in our lives. Here is our text for this chapter:

'This is a faithful saying, and these things I want you to affirm constantly, that those who have believed in God should be careful to maintain good works. These things are good and profitable to men.'

This is one of five pithy sayings which Paul endorses in his pastoral letters to Timothy and Titus - sayings which may well have been current among Christians at that time and which Paul endorses in the words: 'This is a faithful saying'. There's only one of these in his letter to Titus - the one we're looking at right now. Sometimes the words 'this is a faithful saying' introduce what follows, while at other times perhaps they look back to what's just been said.

Here in Titus 3, I suggest that when in verse 8 Paul says 'This is a faithful saying', he's looking back - possibly even back to all of the things that we've been sharing together in this series of studies. The description of the Gospel that's given in these verses we've been looking at from verse 3 forward is so concise yet at the same time so comprehensive that it's very believable to accept that this was an early creed or statement of faith already in use at the time by Christians.

What should be the immediate results that follow from this faithful saying? That those who have believed in God should be careful to maintain good works. So good works come into it, but they're not the root of the Gospel; they're to be the fruit of the Gospel. Or to put it yet another way: good works don't lead to salvation, but they should be the evidence that follows it. Another way of saying this is: it's faith alone that saves us; but the faith that saves us is not alone – works always follow it as the evidence of its reality.

There's a wonderfully brief description of the life of the Lord Jesus given by Peter in Acts chapter 10. Jesus, Peter says, 'went about doing good'. What a testimony that is! What if that were also the outstanding characteristic of every Christian's life! Could we leave behind a better epitaph than that? Surely there could be no better evidence for the truth and reality of the Gospel than if all Christians were Christlike in that they too went about doing good.

In the previous chapter, Titus chapter 2, Paul says of the Lord Jesus in verse 14 that he *'gave Himself for us, that He might redeem us from every lawless deed and purify for Himself His own special people, zealous for good works'*. And there we have it - that one of the specific purposes of Christ's death was that we, as a result, should be keen to do good works. Paul really hammers home this point in his pastoral letters to Timothy and Titus. The expression 'good works' crops up no less than 14 times in the original of these letters. Again and again he stresses it with urgency as at the very end of this letter when he says: *'let our people also learn to maintain good works'*. It all echoes the teaching of the Lord Jesus, of course. Famously, during what we know as his Sermon on the Mount in Matthew 5 and 16, he says: *'Let your light so shine before men, that they may see your good works and glorify your Father in heaven.'*

In Titus, having spoken to older men and women and to slaves, Paul goes on quite generally at the beginning of chapter 3 to say: *'be ready for every good work'*. In First Timothy, he says specifically of women that it is proper for them to be associated with good works (1 Timothy 2:10). When discussing the eligibility of widows in being enrolled to receive support from the church, Paul mentions as one qualification the fact that they should've followed diligently every good work (1 Timothy 5:10). Next, he has a particular message for those who are rich, saying that they should be 'rich in good works, ready to give, willing to share' (1 Timothy 6:18). Christian leaders too, like Titus himself, were expected to be 'a pattern of good works' (Titus 2:7).

Another place in the New Testament where the theme of good works is taken up is in the letter by James. So much so, that some people have mistakenly thought that James is at odds with Paul's teaching. But we must read James' statement that 'a man is justified by works, and not by faith only' in its context. James asks in chapter 2: *'what does it profit... if someone says he has faith but does not have works?'* He then gives the example of someone saying to a starving brother 'be filled' without doing anything practical to help the man. Obviously, that doesn't profit the chap who was starving. So, James concludes, *'faith by itself, if it does not have works, is dead'*. It's important to keep in mind that it's professed faith and not real faith James is discussing here. Remember his opening words in this section? *'If someone says he has faith'* – **says** he has faith. There's a world of difference between someone having real faith and someone who merely professes faith. And that's James' point.

He next imagines this latter kind of person – the kind who simply says he has faith – retorting to the effect that someone can have faith, while someone else can have works – as though these were simply different gifts or roles given by the Lord. But to simply use the language of faith doesn't guarantee that a person is a true believer. The Lord Jesus himself said *'not everyone who says to Me, "Lord, Lord" shall enter the kingdom of heaven'* (Matthew 7:21). James then replies with a challenge: *'Show me your faith without [or apart from] your works, and I will show you my faith by my works.'*

James returns to the attack against the person who merely claims to have faith by pointing out that even the demons acknowledge the existence of God - and then they tremble! - For they'll face the terrible judgement and condemnation of God. Clearly, real faith is much more than head knowledge. And real faith will always have accompanying works with it. What James is contrasting, in a sense, is not so much faith on the one hand and works on the other, but professed faith, mere head knowledge, on the one hand, and on the other hand, real faith demonstrated by works.

It's true that Paul refers to Abraham as someone who was justified by faith while James refers to him as someone justified by works. But the point is they are each referring back to different times and events in the life of Abraham. When Abraham later in life passed God's great test by showing he was prepared to offer up his son Isaac as a sacrifice, he was demonstrating by that very action the reality of the faith he already had. When Paul says we're justified by faith, he uses justified as meaning 'made righteous;' when James says we're justified by our works, he's using the word 'justified' in a different sense: meaning to vindicate. It's the evidence of our works that vindicates our faith, proving its reality.

And here's where we finish our Gospel series with this emphasis on works. Good works are not the basis of our salvation as many wrongly teach, but they are the evidence of it. The evidence of the Gospel in our lives is the good works we do. Faith if it's real will make a difference in the way we live our life. As the old hymn says: 'trust and obey for there's no other way.'

II

... AND THE ERRORS PEOPLE OFTEN MAKE ABOUT IT ...

8

THE ERROR THAT WE CAN FALL AWAY FROM CHRIST

I f the gift of eternal life, once given, doesn't last forever then must we not say that it was never truly 'eternal life' in the first place. That would make it a contradiction in terms, wouldn't it? After all, the Bible in Romans 6:23 says: *"For the wages of sin is death, but the gift of God is eternal life in Christ Jesus our Lord."*

It's overwhelmingly the Bible's teaching that once saved from the penalty of our sins through believing in Christ, we are always saved. In other studies, we explore the New Testament's clear overall teaching on the security of our salvation. This follows the good advice that we need to look at difficult verses in the light of easier, clearer ones – never the other way around. We also need to understand things in the widest context possible. But people do refer to a genuine biblical expression: one that does indeed talk about 'falling away.' However, the relevant question to ask is: 'Falling away from what?' (Especially, once we've established the secure nature of God's gift of salvation to the believer on Christ - underscored as it is by God's sovereign grace.)

Let's examine a couple of difficult verses. They are 1 John 3:15 and Hebrews 6:6. They're among the most common verses which trouble people on this issue. Let's take the reading from John first:

"In this the children of God and the children of the devil are manifest: Whoever does not practice righteousness is not of God, nor is he who does not love his brother. For this is the message that you heard from the beginning, that we should love one another, not as Cain who was of the wicked one and murdered his brother. And why did he murder him? Because his works were evil and his brother's righteous. Do not marvel, my brethren, if the world hates you. We know that we have passed from death to life, because we love the brethren. He who does not love his brother abides in death. Whoever hates his brother is a murderer, and you know that no murderer has eternal life abiding in him. By this we know love, because He laid down His life for us. And we also ought to lay down our lives for the brethren."

There are various wrong views about what these verses mean, for example: 'a true Christian cannot murder, or even hate, his brother;' and 'no murderer can be saved.' The first statement about Christians not hating is sadly not true to experience; and the latter – that no murderer can be saved - is proved wrong by the dying thief who was crucified alongside Jesus. The best way to understand the meaning of the verse which says no murderer has eternal life abiding in him is to read it within the overall context of John's first letter. What was the Apostle John's aim in writing it?

It was to help believers on the Lord Jesus know they were truly saved (see 1 John 5:13: he says, *"that you may know that you have eternal life"*) – it wasn't about how to become a Christian. The Bible's very plain teaching is that works are not the basis of us becoming a Christian – for example, Ephesians 2:8,9 tells us that we're saved by grace through faith and that it's a gift, not the result of works. And the Apostle John is talking here - in his first letter - about works that we need to be doing if we wish to avoid doubting our salvation. We can't lose our salvation, but we can lose our confidence, our assurance of salvation. He gives us 3 ways we can know that we're saved:

1. By maintaining our faith convictions (1 John 2:5)
2. By obeying God's Word & doing what's right (1 John 2:3,29; 3:7,10)
3. And, by loving others (1 John 3:10,14).

The last point refers to what we were saying before: that by loving others we give evidence that we are Christians; and equally, that by hating others we give evidence which denies what we are because it's typically or characteristically non-Christian behaviour - behaviour which is inconsistent and wholly out of place for a believer.

None of this means that Christians aren't capable of hating. And equally, this is not at all saying non-Christians are incapable of loving. Not all followers of Christ obey God's Word and do what's right, not by any means. But the point is this: if we are Christians and wish to live with a level of assurance that we are, then this is what we should be doing: I mean, we should be loving our brothers and doing what the Lord has commanded.

If we hate our brother this will give us no reassurance at all –
either to us or anyone else - that we're Christians. Hatred and
murder typified the way of Cain, the way of the wicked. While
someone is abiding in Christ, and Christ's words are abiding
in them, that person will not be found hating their brothers.
Therefore, John is not saying that a believer who subsequently
commits murder loses his or her salvation – for that was not
his point at all. Remember, what he is saying: act consistently
with your salvation and your confidence will be maintained; act
contrary to what it means to be a believer and you'll have no
reassurance of salvation.

I'd also like us to have a look at Hebrews chapter six and verses
4-8, where we find the expression 'to fall away.' But the key
question again is 'what from?' Let's refresh our memory of this
difficult passage:

"*For it is impossible for those who were once enlightened, and have
tasted the heavenly gift, and have become partakers of the Holy
Spirit, and have tasted the good word of God and the powers of the
age to come, if they fall away, to renew them again to repentance,
since they crucify again for themselves the Son of God, and put
Him to an open shame. For the earth which drinks in the rain that
often comes upon it, and bears herbs useful for those by whom it
is cultivated, receives blessing from God; but if it bears thorns and
briers, it is rejected and near to being cursed, whose end is to be
burned.*"

Once again, if we're going to understand the true meaning of
'falling away' here, it's vital that we see this section within its
true context within the Hebrews' letter. We should be in no

doubt whatsoever that those seen here at great spiritual risk, are true believers, born again persons who have become the target of Satan's attack. For, we read, *"it is impossible for those who were once enlightened, and have tasted the heavenly gift, and have become partakers of the Holy Spirit, and have tasted ... the powers of the age to come, if they fall away, to renew them again to repentance, since they crucify again for themselves the Son of God, and put Him to an open shame."* Clearly, they were born-again people, so what might they fall away from?

An illustration from nature follows, which provides an explanation. Sometimes, when rain falls on the earth, instead of yielding useful, nourishing plants, reflecting God's blessing, it produces thorns and briars, *"near to being cursed, whose end is to be burned"* (vv.7,8). The words, *"whose end is to be burned"* must have brought the readers of this letter up sharply. As with ourselves, it must have led them to reflect on the meaning of such strong statements. We're dealing here with the possibility of believers openly repudiating their faith and profession, so that they exclude themselves from the possibility of repentance. This brings inevitable divine judgement. But is this eternal damnation, as some might be inclined to assume, because of the analogy of the burning of the worthless thorns? No! It is the burning of what the land produces, not of the land itself.

The illustration helps us understand that it's what's produced in a Christian's life that may be one day burned – but by that it ought to be clear that it's his or her works that's meant, and not the believer himself or herself. In other words, the security of our salvation is not compromised – by this passage of scripture, or by any other. We rejoice that we're safe in the Lord's keeping.

None can snatch us out of his hand, as he affirms for us in John 10:28.

For still more confirmation, we can also ask: do we have any other guidance in the New Testament which explains this fearful thought of destruction by burning? Yes, we do, for in 1 Corinthians 3 we've a description of a believer building for God in his or her life, building on the foundation of Jesus Christ a life of service, the value of which may vary widely. Gold, silver, precious stones, wood, hay and stubble are all mentioned. The analogy is with the life of a person whose service is described like this: "*If anyone's work is burned, he will suffer loss; but he himself will be saved, yet so as through fire*" (1 Corinthians 3:15).

At the future, personal assessment of our life of Christian service there will be the possibility of reward or loss of reward depending on our performance. Listen to how the apostle Paul puts it in First Corinthians chapter 3:

"*each one's work will become clear; for the Day will declare it, because it will be revealed by fire; and the fire will test each one's work, of what sort it is. If anyone's work which he has built on it endures, he will receive a reward. If anyone's work is burned, he will suffer loss; but he himself will be saved, yet so as through fire.*

Each Christian is a builder. At the future personal assessment of our Christian service which we'll each have with Christ, there'll be a fiery testing of our works – it'll be the flame test. If it burns, it wasn't any good. Imagine the worst then that could happen for a Christian. They watch all their life's works go up in smoke. They lose, therefore, all their potential reward – there's nothing left for which to be rewarded. Nothing has withstood the fire. But what about the individual concerned? Did you catch Paul's reassuring words in this baseline case? If anyone's work is burned, he will suffer loss; but he himself will be saved, yet so as through fire.

Ah, thank God for that! So then, here's what we are seeing from our Bibles: there are rewards for faithful service that we may fail to gain, as distinct from the gift of salvation itself. Salvation itself is not a reward. It cannot be lost. But we may in some sense 'suffer loss.' That means the loss of potential rewards we may have gained if we'd lived a pleasing life to God's glory.

The judgement-seat of Christ (see also 1 Corinthians 4:5 & 2 Corinthians 510) is an assessment tribunal where we'll receive our Lord's evaluation of how we've served him since the time we first became born-again. It's not about judging us as sinners – for that's dealt with at the cross. It's also not about judging us as sons – for that judging takes place during our lives now (Hebrews 12:5-8). No, the judgement-seat of Christ is only about him judging us as servants.

9

THE ERROR THAT THE GOOD WE DO CAN OUTWEIGH THE BAD (THE BIGGEST LIE IN THE WORLD)

I've heard it said that the author C. S. Lewis, once expressed himself to be amused at the wrongheadedness of those who claimed they could identify the sources of inspiration behind his various writings. And then he added tellingly, "If people get it so wrong on earthly things, what chance do they have with eternal realities?" And people do get it so wrong when they attempt to second-guess eternal realities. 'Do your best,' they say, 'and at the end of life when you stand before God, he'll weigh the good you've done over against the bad, and if the good outweighs the bad, he'll let you into heaven.'

This same basic lie takes a variety of different religious forms, sometimes specifying the good works in question as being certain sacraments or so-called 'pillars' or 'noble truths' or saying that we must pay tithes or observe special days or be baptized – all viewed as qualifying good works towards that final assessment of whether or not we make it into heaven. These are all rejections of the truth. They come about as a result of having considered it, and, in one way or another, found it to be a strange thing. Another author, G. K. Chesterton once said that the truth is always bound to be stranger than fiction - because fiction is something we invent to suit ourselves in order to replace the inconvenient truth which doesn't suit us.

The ultimate reality check, however, comes from the Bible. Even those who may be highly sceptical of the Bible will find its statement in this regard to be consistent with their own personal observations. The Bible declares: *"knowing that a man is not justified by the works of the law but by faith in Jesus Christ, even we have believed in Christ Jesus, that we might be justified by faith in Christ and not by the works of the law; for by the works of the law no flesh shall be justified"* (Galatians 2:16).

This reality, soberly documented as we say in the Bible, and, true to our experience, is telling us, in effect, that: No-one born of a human father in the entire history of the planet has managed to make him or herself acceptable to God based on their own performance of keeping God's rules. That's quite some claim. But where's the evidence to deny it? Think about that for a moment. Take the Ten Commandments.

"And God spoke all these words, saying: "I am the Lord your God, who brought you out of the land of Egypt, out of the house of bondage. "You shall have no other gods before Me. You shall not make for yourself a carved image—any likeness of anything that is in heaven above, or that is in the earth beneath, or that is in the water under the earth; you shall not bow down to them nor serve them. For I, the

Lord your God, am a jealous God, visiting the iniquity of the fathers upon the children to the third and fourth generations of those who hate Me, but showing mercy to thousands, to those who love Me and keep My commandments. You shall not take the name of the Lord your God in vain, for the Lord will not hold him guiltless who takes His name in vain.

Remember the Sabbath day, to keep it holy. Six days you shall labor and do all your work, but the seventh day is the Sabbath of the Lord your God. In it you shall do no work: you, nor your son, nor your daughter, nor your male servant, nor your female servant, nor your cattle, nor your stranger who is within your gates. For in six days the Lord made the heavens and the earth, the sea, and all that is in them, and rested the seventh day. Therefore the Lord blessed the Sabbath day and hallowed it. Honor your father and your mother, that your days may be long upon the land which the Lord your God is giving you. You shall not murder. You shall not commit adultery. You shall not steal. You shall not bear false witness against your neighbor. You shall not covet your neighbor's house; you shall not covet your neighbor's wife, nor his male servant, nor his female servant, nor his ox, nor his donkey, nor anything that is your neighbor's."

It's a lot easier listing them than keeping them! Truth is, we've all broken them. Would anyone dare to make the claim they've never told a lie? And that reminds us of our topic we're exploring: which is the biggest lie in the world. I definitely think it's one of the most popular. In every place and from every background you find some version of the claim that we must do our best, and at the end of life when we stand before God, he'll weigh the good we've done over against the bad, and if the good outweighs the bad, he'll let us get into heaven – or whatever other term is used for heaven.

We really should try to understand that in trying to do good, we're on to a loser. Even if we could strip away all of our vices, it doesn't make us to become good by nature. And, another thing, there's no need to wait until life is over before we learn God's verdict on our life. You can know God's verdict on your performance right now. It's really no secret. The Bible tells us God's advance verdict on each and every one of our lives. It's found in Romans chapter 3:12: and it says, "*There is none who does good*", no, not one.

So, there it is, and we need to listen to it. But, a couple of chapters later in Paul's letter to the Romans we read about the ultimate demonstration of God's love for us (Romans 5:8) – and we discover that there's no need for us to attempt to do anything to get ourselves right with God: for when we were still sinners, Christ died for us. The biblical Christian message is ... Not 'Do!' But 'Done!' This was a message the Apostle Paul was always preaching - wherever he went, and to whomever he wrote. To the Philippian Christians, he wrote:

"Yet indeed I also count all things loss for the excellence of the knowledge of Christ Jesus my Lord, for whom I have suffered the loss of all things, and count them as rubbish, that I may gain Christ and be found in Him, not having my own righteousness, which is from the law, but that which is through faith in Christ, the righteousness which is from God by faith" (Philippians 3:8,9).

Paul wants others to clearly see that his whole way of living had been transformed by his discovery of the supreme value of knowing Christ. This should make it so obvious to others that his claim to be right with God was no longer based on the things of the law that he'd rejected, but his was now a right-standing before God that wasn't his own, it wasn't from the law, but it was by faith only. Next, he writes to Timothy: *"But we know that the law is good if one uses it lawfully, knowing this: that the law is not made for a righteous person, but for the lawless and insubordinate, for the ungodly and for sinners, ... and if there is any other thing that is contrary to sound doctrine, according to the glorious gospel of the blessed God which was committed to my trust"* (1 Timothy 1:8-10).

A Christian is someone who's righteous before God, and the Law is not made for such a person but for the ungodly. The law is designed for sinner, not saint, Paul says. He expands on this in his marvellous explanation of the Gospel in his letter to Christians at Rome: *"Now we know that whatever the law says, it says to those who are under the law, that every mouth may be stopped, and all the world may become guilty before God. Therefore by the deeds of the law no flesh will be justified in His sight, for by the law is the knowledge of sin. But now the righteousness of God apart from the law is revealed, being witnessed by the Law and the Prophets, even the righteousness of God, through faith in Jesus Christ, to all and on all who believe"* (Romans 3:19-22).

Paul makes it clear: the purpose of the Law was to hold us accountable to God whereby we knew we were guilty sinners. At that point the law reaches its terminus (Rom.8:4). Then, as Paul writes to the Galatian Christians, he shows further that the destination is Christ. He says there:

"I do not set aside the grace of God; for if righteousness comes

through the law, then Christ died in vain ... For as many as are of the works of the law are under the curse; for it is written, "Cursed is everyone who does not continue in all things which are written in the book of the law, to do them." But that no one is justified by the law in the sight of God is evident, for "the just shall live by faith." Yet the law is not of faith, but "the man who does them shall live by them. Christ has redeemed us from the curse of the law, having become a curse for us ...

What purpose then does the law serve? It was added because of transgressions, till the Seed should come to whom the promise was made; ... For if there had been a law given which could have given life, truly righteousness would have been by the law. But the Scripture has confined all under sin, that the promise by faith in Jesus Christ might be given to those who believe. But before faith came, we were kept under guard by the law, kept for the faith which would afterward be revealed. Therefore the law was our tutor to bring us to Christ, that we might be justified by faith. But after faith has come, we are no longer under a tutor."

Thank you, Paul, for making the contrast so plain: the works of the law did not and could not save us, but it pointed forward to the faith and faithfulness of the Christ who has! To all of which, let's settle it with the testimony of the writer to the Hebrews, who asks:

"What further need was there that another priest should rise according to the order of Melchizedek, and not be called according to the order of Aaron? For the priesthood being changed, of necessity there is also a change of the law ... on the one hand there is an annulling of the former commandment because of its weakness and

unprofitableness, for the law made nothing perfect; on the other hand, there is the bringing in of a better hope, through which we draw near to God (Hebrews 7:11-19).

10

THE ERROR THAT GOD IS ONLY ONE PERSON

The Trinity is nowhere explicitly stated in Scripture, but is capable of being deduced from it. A classic historical description of the Trinity is 'one God subsisting in three persons and one substance.' To say God is Father, Son and Holy Spirit is entirely biblical; to say that God is 'one substance and three Persons' is an attempt to fit the revelation of God within the limitations of human reason. But reason fails us, and we often turn to analogies. For Augustine, it was love that best illustrated the nature of the Trinity. He said "when I ... love anything, there are three things present: I myself, what I love, and love itself." From this analogy, Augustine argued that God's nature is expressed in a divine community of love. It cannot be said that God is love (1 John 4:8) if God is alone. The Apostle John's declaration that 'God is love' has little real meaning unless God had somebody to love before he created anything, since love involves at least two persons.

Despite its importance, this teaching of the Trinity has never

ceased to be controversial. We need to be careful about the words
we use, recognising their limitations. As we've seen, it seems
we're driven to use analogies. And there's nothing wrong with
that approach, provided we're sensitive to the limitations always
inherent in comparing a thing or a state with the eternal and
limitless God. For example, in Mathematics, the sum of three
infinities is equal in size to a single infinity; this can help us
appreciate that God being three persons does not make him
three gods. Or we may attempt to visualize space with its three
dimensions. 'Space' requires all three, but these dimensions are
not separate 'parts' of the whole, pointing us to the idea of one
God who is a tri-personal or uni-plural being.

A less helpful, and in fact misleading, analogy is that of water,
capable of existing as a gas as well as in liquid and solid forms.
But a danger lurks here, for that may also (and better) be used
to illustrate the false idea of God being only one person who is
capable of existing at any single time in one of three possible
modes. That was a false idea that was around at an early stage
of Christianity. It arose when one man (Sabellius) was trying to
defend against a different error: one that said that Jesus Christ
wasn't fully God. His opponent (Arius, c.250-336) who taught
that about Christ, said that though creator and redeemer, Christ
was not of one substance with the Father, having being born in
time.

That word 'substance' being traded there translates the Greek
word 'hupostasis' (Hebrews 1:3) – from the biblical phrase 'the
image of [God's] substance' (RV) – where it's used in relation to
the nature of Christ. Followers of a man called Arius - one of the
leading characters in the debate- were people who argued that

the Son was not of one and the same substance as the Father - but only of a like or similar substance. They were suggesting that the Son is inferior. The implications of this teaching are obvious and serious. So a Council was held at Nicea in the year 325 AD, resulting in the famous agreed formula describing the Son as '... being of one substance with the Father.' This has stood the test of time, but these remote debates continue to resonate today. Arian interpretations are still put forward by various unitarian groups and by cults. And those Nicean debates still left some loose ends, such as the use of the word 'person' in the context of the Trinity. This word requires cautious use in this context because the normal sense of 'persons' always means individuals with different knowledge, feelings and will. But Father, Son and Spirit all have identical qualities.

The same Council settled the issue of personhood on that earlier word 'substance' (hupostasis) and not on a word for face (prosōpon), based on the then popular idea of actors changing their face masks to represent different characters and personas - which smacks of Sabellian modalism. People holding to the 'one person with three masks' idea of God (or equally 'one element in any of three states') taught that Father, Son and Spirit were only temporary manifestations of the one God, assumed for the purpose of redemption. This error has the apparent virtue of 'simplicity', which is why it's still around today.

There are many instances which make clear the divine nature of the Son and the Spirit, as both sharing the attributes of the Father. One particularly noteworthy example is the Great Commission (Matthew 28:19), where the risen Lord commands disciples to baptise in one name – the singular name of God –

but belonging to all three persons of Father, Son and Holy Spirit. Clearly, the Trinity is also seen before the Incarnation. Even in the uncompromising monotheism of Deuteronomy 6:4, the word 'echad' describes 'one' God: and this particular word for 'one' doesn't mean one in isolation, but one in unity, for example as in a bunch of grapes or one people. It means a composite unity – as in Genesis 2:24 where husband and wife together combine to become 'one flesh'. In contrast, the word for absolute unity in the sense of a single oneness is 'yachīd.' This is never used for God in the Bible.

In the New Testament, it's not surprising to find the work of the Trinity particularly evident in Christ's incarnation, baptism and resurrection and in the act of atonement, as we'll go on to see. Some cults, and groups known as 'Oneness' groups, like to point out that the word 'Trinity' is not found in the Bible. That's correct, but the doctrine can be deduced from the following clear teachings of Scripture: there is only one God (Deuteronomy 6:4, Isaiah 44:8) where the Hebrew word for 'one' is the word for a bunch of grapes type of unity. The Father is called God (John 6:27, Ephesians 4:6). The Son is called God (Hebrews 1:8). The Holy Spirit is called God (Acts 5:3–4), and is not some impersonal force, but a person (Acts 13:2). They are distinct, e.g. at the baptism of Jesus in Matthew 3:16–17 all three were simultaneously present in a distinct way. The distinction in persons within the one God means that it is possible for Jesus to be the 'one Mediator between God and men' (1 Timothy 2:5). It also makes the substitutionary atonement possible. Jesus said that his Father sent him (John 14:24) and that the Spirit was sent by both the Father (John 14:26) and the Son (John 16:7).

One of the most beautiful and comforting of Scriptures is surely the apostolic blessing, mentioning the love of God, the grace of Christ, and the fellowship of the Holy Spirit (2 Corinthians 13:14). This points us towards different emphases of the work of each person, as glimpsed in the work of creation, for example, but ascribing fixed roles may be too restrictive. For example, there are aspects by which all three persons abide within the heart of the believer. We may safely summarise that there are particular (but not exclusive) focuses of the respective persons of the Trinity.

It's natural for us to see in the term 'son' an indication of subordination and generation of being. But what lies behind the idea of sonship in biblical speech is 'likeness'; whatever the father is, that is what the son is also. When thinking in terms of God, this strongly asserts the Son's equality with the Father. The adjective translated as 'only begotten' (John 1:14; 3:16-18; 1 John 4:9) really adds only the idea of uniqueness (see Luke 7:12; 8:42; 9:39: Hebrews 11:17). In John 5:18 we read: *"the Jews sought all the more to kill Him, because He not only broke the Sabbath, but also said that God was His Father, making Himself equal with God."*

Jesus was, rightly, understood to be calling God 'his *own* Father (ESV),' that is, using the terms 'father' and 'son' not in a merely figurative sense - as when Israel was called God's son - but in the real sense: that is, in actual fact. To be the Son of God in any sense was to be like God in that sense; to be God's *own* Son was to be exactly like God, to be fully 'equal with God.' Similarly, we read in 1 Corinthians 2:10,11: *"... the Spirit searches all things, yes, the deep things of God. For what man knows the things of a*

*man except the spirit of the man which is in him? Even so no one
knows the things of God except the Spirit of God."* Here the Spirit
appears as the innermost essence of God's Being. As the spirit
of man is the very life of man, so the Spirit of God appears as
his life-element, as it were. How can he be supposed, then, to
be subordinate to God, or to derive his Being from God? (In
whatever ordering our finite minds think of for the persons of
the Trinity, we should be prepared to think as much in horizontal
terms, as in hierarchical terms).

There is, of course, no question that in how God operates, for
example, in redemption, the principle of subordination among
persons of the Trinity is expressed. The Father is first, the Son is
second, and the Spirit is third in those operations by which our
salvation is accomplished. Whatever the Father does, he does
through the Son (Romans 2:16;3:22;5:1,11,17,21; Ephesians 1:5; 1
Thessalonians 5:9; Titus 3:5), and by the Spirit. The Son is sent
by the Father and does his Father's will (John 6:38); the Spirit is
sent by the Son and doesn't speak from himself, but only takes
what belongs to Christ and shows it to his people (John 17:7 ff.).

But it's not clear that the same principle of subordination applies
at a more fundamental level. After all, the operational relations
of subordination may be due to a voluntary agreement between
the persons of the Trinity, by virtue of which a distinct role in the
work of redemption is assumed by each. We can certainly agree
on what has to be our final point, specifically on the actions of
the Trinity in the Incarnation of our Lord for the purpose of our
redemption: *"great is the mystery of godliness"* (1 Timothy 3:16)!

11

THE ERROR THAT GOD'S SPIRIT IS ONLY AN IMPERSONAL INFLUENCE

T he words of the Lord Jesus in John 14 give us an appreciation of how radical a development it was when the Spirit of God first began to reside in human lives. It's something specific to this Church Age - and by 'this Church Age' we mean the period that began with the descent of the Holy Spirit at the Pentecost event in Acts chapter 2. In John 14 verse 17 while speaking to his disciples, the Lord Jesus said: *"the Father ... will give you another Helper ... the Spirit of truth, whom the world cannot receive, because it neither sees Him nor knows Him; but you know Him, for He dwells with you and will be in you."*

Notice the Lord's words: He dwells with you and will be in you. Right up to that time in the history of God's dealings with people, his Spirit had come upon certain of them at different times for special purposes, for example the Spirit of the LORD had come upon Samson when performing his heroic exploits. But these, it seems, were periods of temporary residence. The Holy Spirit didn't permanently indwell - or reside in - these people. In his upper room ministry, the Lord Jesus signalled that a remarkable change was going to come into effect when, speaking about the Spirit, he said to his disciples: *"He dwells with you and will be in you."* In their service for God previously, these disciples had known the Spirit with them, notably when they were empowered to heal and cast out demons. But now - and the Lord was anticipating Pentecost - the Holy Spirit was going to be permanently in residence within them. Their bodies were to become temples of the Holy Spirit, as Paul later taught the Corinthian believers.

This is a truth that's characteristic of this age we're living in - characteristic that is for believers on the Lord Jesus, of course. Why the change? Why now the permanent indwelling through the Spirit of God? The Lord was going away: by means of the cross he was going to return to heaven. He promised not to leave his followers as orphans. He said: *"I will come to you"* (v.18). This was his coming in the Holy Spirit, fulfilled from Pentecost. In and through the indwelling Spirit he promised that his disciples of this age would see him even though the world couldn't. Doesn't that show us clearly that the Lord's purpose in sending the Spirit to live permanently now in every true believer is so as to make Christ's presence real to us through communion?

We can't write like Shakespeare, for we don't have his genius, but what's more wonderful is that we can know, and become like, Christ, because we have his Spirit - for the Holy Spirit is the Spirit of Christ. And he makes him real to us in our daily reading of Scripture, as real to us as he was to the 12 disciples when he was physically here. We should read verses 9 to 11 of Romans 8 on this topic that concerns the Spirit's most fundamental ministry – the fact that he lives in us, making these bodies of ours his permanent dwelling-place. This is what these verses say: *"But you are not in the flesh but in the Spirit, if indeed the Spirit of God dwells in you. Now if anyone does not have the Spirit of Christ, he is not His. And if Christ is in you, the body is dead because of sin, but the Spirit is life because of righteousness. But if the Spirit of Him who raised Jesus from the dead dwells in you, He who raised Christ from the dead will also give life to your mortal bodies through His Spirit who dwells in you."*

God's Spirit who dwells in you – that's our theme. And did you notice in the reading that the Spirit is called the Spirit of Christ and the Spirit of him that raised Jesus from the dead, that is the Spirit of the Father? The LORD our God is one, one God, but expressed in three persons: Father, Son and Spirit. What an indwelling this is! This is how the Scripture can say: *"Christ in you, the hope of glory."* Christ is in us through his Spirit. Let's specially note the force of what we've read: that if someone isn't indwelt by God's Spirit, then they don't belong to Christ. All who belong to Christ by saving faith, have, without exception, received the indwelling Spirit, the Bible teaches. This isn't an option or even a later blessing only for a few. No, just as Christ is now physically absent from all believers here, so he has sent his Spirit to be in each and every believer.

The Lord Jesus described the Holy Spirit as *"another Helper"* in the place we were reading from in John 14. The word 'helper' comes from a word meaning to draw alongside. Isn't that precious teaching? Often, we struggle with truth we can't fully understand, at other times with troubling personal and spiritual concerns - in all these and at all times we have someone alongside us to help us. And that someone is God's Spirit. How gracious of him to make these poor hearts of ours his home! And he's always at hand just when we need him, he's always alongside - for he's permanently residing in our hearts.

With such a holy Guest, we have to remember not to grieve him - he's a person, not simply an influence as many wrongly teach - he's a person with emotions just as the Bible equally speaks of him having a 'mind' (Romans 8:27) and a 'will' (1 Corinthians 12:11). That's why Ephesians 4 verse 30 says: *"Do not grieve the Holy Spirit of God"* and mentions corrupt or unwholesome speech as an example of something that will grieve him. It's important to be totally clear that the Holy Spirit is a person. All the elements of personality can be detected in scriptures that apply to him. Romans 8:27 tells us about his 'mind'; Ephesians 4:30, as just mentioned, informs us that he has 'feelings'; while 1 Corinthians 12:11 mentions his 'will'.

In the early part of Acts 5, we find the tragic story of Ananias and Sapphira, two early Christian disciples. Peter tells us they'd lied to the Holy Spirit. Let's read it together: *"But a certain man named Ananias, with Sapphira his wife, sold a possession. And he kept back part of the proceeds, his wife also being aware of it, and brought a certain part and laid it at the apostles' feet. But Peter said, 'Ananias, why has Satan filled your heart to lie to the Holy Spirit and keep back part of the price of the land for yourself? While it remained, was it not your own? And after it was sold, was it not in your own control? Why have you conceived this thing in your heart? You have not lied to men but to God.' Then Ananias, hearing these words, fell down and breathed his last. So great fear came upon all those who heard these things."*

These verses also imply the personhood of the Holy Spirit. You can't lie to a mere abstract influence (as some cults claim the Holy Spirit is). But this same section goes much further and makes plain they'd not lied to man, but to God. This clarifies that the Holy Spirit is a divine person, a member of the Godhead. This is why Hebrews 9:14 can describe him as *"the eternal Spirit"* - who is omnipresent (present everywhere: Psalm 139:7) and omniscient (all-knowing: 1 Corinthians 2:10,11). Since he indwells us, and our bodies are temples of the Holy Spirit, we're to glorify God with our bodies. On a practical level that would seem to rule out pursuits and habits that are harmful to our bodies.

Shall I quote it in full? End of First Corinthians chapter 6, isn't it? These are the three 'do you not know's?' - Paul's probing questions, and all dealing with our bodies, the members of Christ. The final 'do you not know?' is this one: *"Or do you not know that your body is the temple of the Holy Spirit who is in you, whom you have from God, and you are not your own? For you were bought at a price; therefore glorify God in your body and in your spirit, which are God's"* (vv.19-20). God help us to do just that. Finally, we repeat the main reason why the Spirit comes to live in us from the moment of our conversion: it's so that he might make the Lord Jesus Christ real to us through day to day communion, and our responsibility is to glorify God in these bodies of ours in which he, too, dwells.

12

THE ERROR THAT WE CAN LOSE OUR SALVATION

God wants us to fully rejoice in his gift of eternal life, and his blessings of peace and joy (Romans 15:13). John wrote, *"These things I have written to you who believe in the name of the Son of God, that you may know that you have eternal life, and that you may continue to believe in the name of the Son of God"* (1 John 5:13).

Some, however, teach the false doctrine that the Christian believer can be saved and then lost again. This error is the result of confusing salvation with service. If you read 1 Corinthians 9:24-27 where the Apostle Paul talks about the possibility of being disqualified, you'll see that Paul's not talking about God's gift of salvation, but about serving the Lord by staying legitimately in contention for a prize – in the same way as an athlete needs to remain within the rules of the competition so as not to be barred from it. We can't compete to earn eternal life, because it's a gift. But after we've received the gift, Christians strive to serve well to earn the reward of an eternal crown. While we can be disqualified from that prize, it doesn't affect our eternal life.

Believers are children of God because they're born of God. Our heavenly Father may be disillusioned by our behaviour and our service, but we can never cease to be his children. We ask again, can disbelief, or an act of misconduct, or committing a crime, or any other thing rob anyone of the salvation that's found in Christ? No, but it's not a new assertion to say that a backslider may lose his or her salvation, for the Apostle Paul evidently debated with those who claimed just that. They raised the objection to Paul's preaching which is implied by the opening words of Romans chapter 6: *"What shall we say then? Shall we continue in sin that grace may abound?"*

In other words, Paul must have been preaching 'once saved, always saved,' because of the fact that some were clearly reacting against it back then, saying: 'Come on, Paul, do you really mean to say that someone who's known salvation by placing personal faith in Christ can then live carelessly without any fear of losing his or her salvation?' 'If that's the case,' they argued, 'we might as well all sin at every opportunity if that means it gives God more opportunities to be gracious in forgiving our many sins!'

In that 6th chapter of Romans, Paul shows how wrong-headed this point of view is. He replies by saying: *"Certainly not! How shall we who died to sin live any longer in it?"* (Romans 6:2). This is the basis of Paul's rejection of their 'we may as well live as we please' philosophy. He tells them that the reality is that the believer on the Lord Jesus Christ has in fact *"died to sin."* But what does this mean? Paul also tells us that *"Christ died to sin."*

There must be a consistency between what it means for Christ to die to sin, and what it means for the believer to die to sin - since both these expressions are used in the same place in our Bible.

Paul reasons that, if Christ died to sin, and if we're identified with Christ, then it follows that we, too, died to sin – and as a practical consequence it would be out of place for us to now lead a life dominated by sinful practices. That's the sense of the flow of this paragraph in our Bibles. And to prove that we really have been identified with Christ, Paul shares two things: a revelation of what happened at our conversion, and an explanation of the meaning of our water baptism. First, it's at salvation, when by God's grace we are saved through faith, that we were identified with the Christ of the cross in his death and resurrection. When we believe, it's as if Christ's death becomes our death and it's then that we receive new life in Christ. Later, in water baptism we demonstrate that fact by 'acting it out' – i.e., by being buried in water and rising again. Water baptism is only a symbolic witness to all who watch it – symbolic of our previous identification with a crucified and resurrected saviour.

There are so many ways of assuring ourselves biblically of our eternal security in Christ, but the one that I personally find the most persuasive is the fact that the Bible teaches us that the primary salvation decision is God's not ours - which means that any view which permits us to lose our salvation seriously underplays God's sovereignty. Jesus invited people to come to him and to rest in the knowledge of sins forgiven. In itself that famous invitation at the end of Matthew chapter 11 invites people to stop relying on their own efforts to obtain salvation, and simply come and rest in the salvation which Christ is offering as a gift. But in John chapter 6, the Lord pulls the curtain further back to reveal something of the bigger picture of what's involved in a sinner coming to Christ.

He says: *"All that the Father gives Me will come to Me, and the one who comes to Me I will [a] by no means cast out ... No one can come to Me unless the Father who sent Me draws him"* (John 6:37,44). So, standing behind our coming to Christ in personal faith, is God's sovereign choice of each one of us who believes on the Lord Jesus. We find additional clarity on this point in the letter to the Ephesians, and its opening verses: *"Blessed be the God and Father of our Lord Jesus Christ, who has blessed us with every spiritual blessing in the heavenly places in Christ, just as He chose us in Him before the foundation of the world, that we should be holy and without blame before Him in love"* (Ephesians 1:3-4).

A moment's reflection ought to show us that if these things are so - if the matter of our salvation and eternal destiny has been of concern to God from before the foundation of the world - then it's highly unlikely that we should be able to toss it away on a whim – or even by a quite deliberate later rejection. Loss of faith in a believer is tragic, and brings about a loss of enjoyment of the assurance of salvation, but salvation itself as God's sovereign gift remains, having been underwritten by God's own choice from before this universe came into being. The outcome is already finalized in God's purpose (Ephesians 2:6; Romans 8:30) – as far as God is concerned it's as if we're already seated and glorified with Christ!

"You have become estranged from Christ, you who attempt to

be justified by law; you have fallen from grace." These strong
words are found in Galatians 5:4. This was Paul's answer to
those who'd been saved through faith, prior to wondering if
they should then bolster it with circumcision. This passage
is decisive as to the fact that there can be no mixture of any
kind between grace and works. Works don't come into the
obtaining of salvation; nor are they regarded as necessary for
holding on to salvation afterwards. But sometimes these verses
have been distorted in their meaning and made to suggest quite
the opposite of Paul's argument: that we can be estranged or
severed from Christ and fall away from grace in the sense of the
loss of our actual salvation!

That's not at all what Paul's saying here. Instead, he says, pure
reliance on Christ on the one hand, and the desire to depend
in some way on human effort on the other, belong in totally
different categories - such that seeking to even maintain our
salvation by some effort of our own transfers us from the one
'camp' to the other. In that sense, we're cut off from being able
to proclaim 'Christ alone.' We've fallen away from the advocacy
of 'grace alone.' By no longer operating in the sphere of 'Christ
alone' and 'grace alone,' we lose all certainty and enjoyment of
the salvation God's provided for us in the one finished work of
his own son upon the cross (John 19:30).

Of course, this is what Paul consistently taught. You remember
he taught the Philippian jailor *"believe on the Lord Jesus Christ
and you will be saved,"* but just suppose for a moment that the
gift of salvation is subsequently conditional upon our own good
works - then we can't possibly know if we've done well enough
to still keep hold of it or not – and so Paul's note of confident

assurance to the jailor - *"you will be saved"* - would then ring false. When a person professes faith in Christ (as Peter did) s/he is built by Christ into his Church and is in fact baptized by Christ in the Holy Spirit into that Church which is known biblically as Christ's Body. This is the Lord's action, and confirmed by the stated fact that the greatest known power could not overpower Christ's Church. We should check that again, it comes from the Lord's words in Matthew 16:18 – here they are once more: *"I will build My church, and the gates of Hades shall not prevail against it."*

Did you get that? After confirming his identity to Peter while at Caesarea Philippi, Christ proceeded to state the glorious purpose he was about – namely building his Church, comprised of all true believers of this age of grace (from the cross until Jesus' return). Then he added that nothing, not even the greatest power known to the ancient world, the power of death and the underworld, could defeat this great divine purpose. Psalm 16:10 prophesied that Christ's soul in death went down into Sheol or Hades, the realm of the dead. But the same disciple Peter says later in his preaching to the Jews in Acts chapter 2 (v.24) that Jesus couldn't possibly be held there in death, but God raised him up. If God hadn't raised up Christ from the dead, if the gates of Hades had not been forced to yield for him, then this great Church-building purpose of the ages would've been overpowered – but it wasn't, nor could it be! Praise God for that!

Surely this fact of the gates of Hades and death not being able to overpower Christ's purpose in his Church precludes any such notion as the dis-memberment of a single believer from that Body, that Church. Who's going to mutilate Christ's Body?! Our place in the Body of Christ is absolutely secured at conversion. In the same way that we might make use of recognized landmarks in giving someone directions, it's just as necessary to identify the Bible's landmark teachings and then navigate our way around individual and sometimes difficult verses. If our understanding of a particular text seems to be at odds with one of the Bible's main teachings, it may indicate that the text should be related to a different line of teaching instead.

One such landmark teaching is that a truly born-again person, through faith in Jesus, is secure in God's keeping so far as his salvation from eternal judgement is concerned. Such a person is seen as 'in Christ.' But there's another equally clear landmark teaching which is that as the believer travels daily nearer his assured heavenly home he or she is accountable to the Lord Jesus for their response to the will of God. These two landmark biblical teachings are distinct but complementary. One line gives the believer assurance of salvation from his deserved eternal judgement in the lake of fire; but the other establishes that such grace in salvation mustn't be lightly regarded. We need to add on our part all diligence, in our faith supplying virtue, knowledge, self-control, patience, godliness and love of the brethren (2 Peter 1:5-8).

13

THE ERROR THAT CHRIST WAS NO MORE THAN A MAN

I'm sure you've heard many arguments put forward by people who've stumbled in their understanding over either the deity of Christ or else they've stumbled over failing to acknowledge his full humanity. Jesus Christ is the unique god-man – that's our total conviction based on the Bible as the Word of God, declaring to us the full deity of the actual man Jesus Christ. It was the so-called 'council of Nicea,' a gathering of religious scholars, that affirmed the sixty-six books of the Bible as we have them today; and it also endorsed the understanding of the triune nature of God as Father, Son and Holy Spirit. But it was left to a later council, the Council of Chalcedon in 451 AD to affirm that Jesus Christ is fully God and fully man. This, then, is a debate with some history.

Of course, the Scriptures themselves already teach us those things, and they really should be beyond dispute. These historical debates simply involved people trying to do justice to the teaching of the Word of God. Jesus Christ certainly is both fully God and fully man. Some years ago, when my son Michael was still a boy, we had a camping holiday on the outskirts of Paris and one day went to see the tomb of Napoleon Bonaparte. It's a very impressive sight, but it did remind me of something much more impressive associated with Napoleon - some of the things that he said in the years after 1815, and after the Battle of Waterloo. He was exiled on Elba and had time to think and reflect, and he spoke to some of the counts and generals who were with him and asked, "What do you think, gentlemen, about Jesus Christ?"

Their answer was somewhat non-committal, so Napoleon volunteered what he thought of Jesus Christ. He said 'Christ alone has succeeded in raising the spirit of man to such a point that it becomes insensible to time and space. Across a chasm of 1,800 years Jesus Christ asks something that is very difficult - he demands the human heart and forthwith it is granted. Wonderful,' Napoleon said, 'that in defiance of time and space, the spirit of man with all his powers and faculty becomes an annexation of the Empire of Christ.' Napoleon contrasted that with himself. He said, 'I know what it is to command the allegiance of an army and to have people who will swear unswerving devotion to me.' But he was no shrinking violet, he said, and 'in order to achieve that I had to stand before them with the electric influence of my looks and my words and my voice.' He could command the allegiance of other men by being present with them and standing before them. But, he said, it's altogether different with Jesus Christ – 'over a chasm of 1,800 years, he demands that which is most extraordinary: that unconditionally the human heart be granted to him and forthwith it is.' He then concluded that this phenomenon is unaccountable other than if someone should believe in the absolute divinity of Jesus Christ.

It's sometimes said that Jesus never claimed to be God. I want you to consider if that's an accurate assessment, based on how the second chapter of Mark's Gospel opens ...

"And again He entered Capernaum after some days, and it was heard that He was in the house. Immediately many gathered together, so that there was no longer room to receive them, not even near the door. And He preached the word to them. Then they came to Him, bringing a paralytic who was carried by four men. And when they could not come near Him because of the crowd, they uncovered the roof where He was. So when they had broken through, they let down the bed on which the paralytic was lying. When Jesus saw their faith, He said to the paralytic, "Son, your sins are forgiven you."

And some of the scribes were sitting there and reasoning in their hearts, "Why does this Man speak blasphemies like this? Who can forgive sins but God alone?" But immediately, when Jesus perceived in His spirit that they reasoned thus within themselves, He said to them, "Why do you reason about these things in your hearts? Which is easier, to say to the paralytic, 'Your sins are forgiven you,' or to say, 'Arise, take up your bed and walk'? But that you may know that the Son of Man has power on earth to forgive sins"—He said to the paralytic, "I say to you, arise, take up your bed, and go to your house." Immediately he arose, took up the bed, and went out in the presence of them all, so that all were amazed and glorified God, saying, "We never saw anything like this!" (Mark 2:1-12).

Surely there could not have been a more emphatic way for Jesus to press his claim to be fully God as well as fully human. He affirmed only God can forgive sins – and then proceeded to forgive someone's sins! The Jews that day definitely understood his claim. It's natural for us to regard the term 'son' as implying subordination. But what lies behind the idea of sonship in biblical speech is simply the idea of 'likeness'; whatever the father is, the son is also. When thinking in terms of God, this asserts the son's equality with the father rather than his subordination. The adjective 'only begotten' or 'one and only' (John 1:14;3:16-18;1 John 4:9) adds only the idea of uniqueness (see Luke 7:12; 8:42; 9:38; Hebrews 11:17).

In John 5:18 we read: *"Therefore the Jews sought all the more to kill Him, because He not only broke the Sabbath, but also said that God was His Father, making Himself equal with God."* Jesus was, rightly, understood to call God *"his own Father"* (ESV) that is, to use the terms father and son not in a merely figurative sense, as when Israel was called God's son, but in their real sense. To be the son of God in any sense was to be like God in that sense; to be God's *own* Son was to be exactly like God, to be 'equal with God.' So, once again, as in Mark 2, the Jews definitely understood Jesus to be claiming to be exactly like God. This was also made clear at his trial: *"The high priest asked Him, saying to Him, "Are You the Christ, the Son of the Blessed?" Jesus said, "I am. And you will see the Son of Man sitting at the right hand of the Power, and coming with the clouds of heaven." Then the high priest tore his clothes and said, "What further need do we have of witnesses? You have heard the blasphemy!* (Mark 14:61-63).

Allow me to ask you to compare two readings: first, one from John 9:38 and then the other taken from Revelation 19:10. Then I'm going to ask you to draw your own conclusion. First from

John 9, and the healing of the man born blind:

"Jesus heard that they had cast him out; and when He had found him, He said to him, "Do you believe in the Son of God?" He answered and said, "Who is He, Lord, that I may believe in Him?" And Jesus said to him, "You have both seen Him and it is He who is talking with you." Then he said, "Lord, I believe!" And he worshiped Him" (John 9:35-38). And now from Revelation 19, at a point where an angel is speaking to the Apostle John in a vision: " ... *And he said to me, "These are the true sayings of God." And I fell at his feet to worship him. But he said to me, "See that you do not do that! I am your fellow servant, and of your brethren who have the testimony of Jesus. Worship God! For the testimony of Jesus is the spirit of prophecy."* (Revelation 19:9,10).

The difference between these two incidents, allows us to see very clearly that whereas the worship of an angel, far less a man, is not permitted; Jesus did accept worship. That's another way in which he makes a very definite claim to being divine. Added to all this, we have Titus 2:13 where we read of Jesus described as being both our *"great God"* and *"our ... Savior"* when it reads: *"our great God and Savior Jesus Christ."* And for the writer to the Hebrews, Jesus is addressed (by the application of Old Testament scripture) not only as 'Lord' (Hebrews 1:10) but actually as 'God' (Hebrews 1:8).

But, equally, there's no New Testament writer who more emphatically underlines Jesus' humanity than the writer to the Hebrews whom we've just quoted – and who also tells us: *"Inasmuch then as the children have partaken of flesh and blood, He Himself likewise shared in the same, that through death"* he

83

might release or deliver them (Hebrews 2:14). *"In all things He had to be made like his brethren"* if he was to be their effective high priest. He sympathizes with the weaknesses of his fellow-men and knows how best to help them, for *"He Himself has suffered, being tempted"* - tempted indeed *"in all points ... as we are, yet without sin"* (Hebrews 2:18; 4:15). There's everything appealingly human in the picture of one who poured out his soul in *"prayers and supplications, with vehement cries and tears, to Him who was able to save him from death,"* and *"learned obedience by the things which He suffered"* (Hebrews 5:7,8) - who blazed the trail of faith and persevered to the end, enduring the cross and despising the shame (see Hebrews 12:1,2).

The reality of Christ's humanity is on display here. And for good reason: another ancient misunderstanding was called Docetism, from a Greek word meaning 'to seem.' This early heresy questioned Jesus' humanity – saying he only seemed to be human. This is equally in error, but has tended to be more tolerated – as when some say that from conception to birth our Lord passed through the body of his mother 'like water through a pipe', deriving no part of his humanity from her. To defend against such a view, how wonderfully precise the inspired writing of the Apostle Paul is when he says: *"For what the Law could not do, in that it was weak through the flesh, God did by sending His own Son in the likeness of sinful flesh, on account of sin: He condemned sin in the flesh"* (Romans 8:3). Our Lord did not come in the mere likeness of flesh; far less in sinful flesh; but *"in the likeness of sinful flesh"* – fully human as we are (which, as our kinsman redeemer, was required of him), but without sin and indeed incapable of it.

All in all, there's no other hope but in God's Son, Jesus Christ - the only one in whom we may have hope for now and for eternity - one who's fully God and fully man.

14

THE ERROR THAT BAPTISM IN WATER IS NECESSARY FOR SALVATION

As I was preparing to share this study, I was in a country where people believe in and practice 'baptismal regeneration.' In case you haven't encountered this, it's the belief that baptism in water (as distinct from baptism in the Holy Spirit, Matthew 3:11; 1 Corinthians 12:13) is necessary for someone to become a child of God; the belief that it's required for them to have new life. In other words, this teaching says that you need to be baptized in water in order to obtain salvation from the penalty of your sins. In checking that out, let's come afresh to our Bibles. We'll aim to show - from Romans chapter 6, for example, - that believers' water baptism is a public recognition of an inner change – one that's been previously brought about by God through faith on our part. Upon baptism - and in recognition of his or her union with Christ - the Christian believer resolves to live to please the Lord.

I well remember my first attempt at outlining orthodox New Testament teaching on Philippine soil. It was June 2003 and the room was comfortably full with some 40-50 persons giving rapt attention, all with their Bibles open. I was speaking through an interpreter and this, although accurately done, elongated the process. The feature, however, that really lengthened the study was its highly interactive nature. I was still covering 'first base' on the New Birth when the first interruption came. '"*Born of water and the Spirit*" (John 3:5), someone shouted out: 'Doesn't this refer to believer's baptism in water; and doesn't it prove that such a baptism is required if we're to be re-born? And only in this way, after baptism, we possess salvation from the penalty of our sins?'

It shouldn't seem strange to us that we should meet this opinion. It has a long history, stretching back, it would seem, at least as far as the years 110-165 AD and the time of Justin Martyr who wrote: 'He [who] will not be baptized, shall be condemned as an unbeliever ... For the Lord says: "Except a man be baptized of water and of the Spirit, he shall by no means enter into the kingdom of heaven"' (Justin Martyr, Constitutions of the Holy Apostles, Ante-Nicene Fathers, vol.7, p.456-457). Speaking in another place of those under instruction, he said: 'Then we bring them to a place where there is water, and they are regenerated in the same manner in which we ourselves were regenerated' (Justin, First Apology, chap. 61).

The problem with this interpretation of John 3:5 – where we read about "*born of water and the Spirit*" - is that it makes a wrong assumption that "*born of water*" refers to water baptism. Is there a better way of understanding the Lord's combined use of water and the Spirit in relation to the necessary spiritual renewing of our nature in preparation for the kingdom of God? There is, for in verse 10 of the same chapter, John 3, Jesus challenges Nicodemus' ignorance of the relevant Old Testament background which he clearly expected Nicodemus to have, since he was described as *"the teacher of Israel"* (by the Lord). From the Old Testament, we can compare another reference to 'water' and 'spirit' that's found in Ezekiel's writing: *"I will sprinkle clean **water** on you, and you will be clean ... and put a new **spirit** within you; and I will remove the heart of stone from your flesh and give you a heart of flesh"* (Ezekiel 36:25,26).

It's a very similar context of inner spiritual transformation – but this one is a national one, involving Israel. It's a direct linking of 'water' or 'washing' to the Spirit's work at the time of (Israel's future) conversion. It's helpful to see this, because it strongly suggests that the wording of Titus 3:5 – where it talks of: *"the washing of regeneration and renewing of the Holy Spirit"*- it strongly suggests this is the better clarification of 'water' in John 3:5. In other words, it's not describing baptism at all.

After that first encounter in Davao city, I've repeatedly come across those of different denominations who advocate that, without water baptism, we simply can't be assured of divine forgiveness and a place in heaven. Some others stumble over Acts 2:38. Surely, they say, this verse which talks of being *"baptized ... for the remission (forgiveness) of ... sins"* in order to *"receive the gift of the Holy Spirit"* is all the proof we need that baptismal regeneration is an essential part of the established New Testament pattern of teaching?

However, before we could ever conclude that, we must first apply the safeguard of comparing scripture with scripture, allowing verses where the meaning is plain to clarify our understanding of texts where the meaning is in dispute. When we do that, it's most likely that the verse we've mentioned in Acts 2:38 was some kind of special requirement to attest to the genuineness of the faith commitment of those particular Jews; the reason being that they belonged to the generation who had put Christ to death on the cross. When we compare Acts 10:43 & 48 later in our Bibles, and also Acts 19:2 & 5, the settled pattern of Apostolic teaching becomes very clear: in each case the forgiveness of sins and receiving the gift of the Holy Spirit are plainly said to be given to those who believe, before their water baptism.

Paul sends a clear signal in 1 Corinthians 1:17 by saying: *"Christ did not send me to baptize, but to preach the gospel."* If it is taught that baptism is necessary for salvation, how could Paul make such an emphatic distinction? Usually, advocates of the belief that baptism in water is necessary for salvation rest their case strongly on Mark 16:16. If only subjected to a superficial review, this verse seems to make their case clearly: *"He who believes and is baptized shall be saved; but he who does not believe will be condemned."* But if anyone wishes to argue on the basis of this verse, they must be faced up with the second part of it which focuses on the critical element of belief alone among those who are not to be condemned. I often point out that I, too, am a baptized believer and I know that I am saved, but the Scriptures (including this one) teach that it's crucially my faith in Christ's atoning death that has saved me from future condemnation before a holy God.

It's also worthwhile pointing out that the concluding section of Mark's Gospel – of which this verse is part – is not found in early New Testament manuscripts. As a result, we can by no means be certain that this is part of the inspired original text. It's foolhardy to base a doctrine upon a singular text whose authority can, at least, be debated. Usually, as the debate unfolds, there comes an anticipated appeal to 1 Peter 3:21 (NASB) which says: "*Corresponding to* [those brought safely through the waters of Noah's flood], *baptism now saves you - not the removal of dirt from the flesh, but an appeal to God for a good conscience.* It's necessary to think rather carefully here. At the time of the devastating, worldwide Flood in the days of Noah, the ark was the vehicle to save its occupants from the watery judgment; but the waters themselves were the vehicle which saved the very same persons from the previous corrupt world. The former seems to typify or picture salvation from the penalty of sins; and the latter, pictures salvation from a corrupting society in which we may in all good conscience have to endure suffering when doing what's right. Only in this last sense does – or can – baptism be said (correctly) to 'save' us. A baptized follower of the Lord Jesus can helpfully consult their conscience regarding their intended actions: is this activity consistent with my advertised identity as a follower of Christ?

And alongside this, Acts 22:16 can be satisfactorily shown to be in full agreement. Let's look at the verse: "*... be baptized, and wash away your sins.*" Set at the time of Saul's dramatic conversion, these are the words of God's servant, Ananias. Saul had encountered the risen Christ on the Damascus highway. He too, had been a high profile opponent of the Christian persuasion, and it might be argued (as in Acts 2:38) that the public act of water baptism was accordingly and again exceptionally required of him. It's not necessary, however, to understand the text in that specialized way, but we can view it here in a way that applies to all believers. For believer's baptism is intended to be a watershed event in each of our lives (Romans 6:4; cf. 1 Peter 3:21). By saving faith, we are not the same person we once were in God's sight (Romans 6:6), and following our water baptism we are not to live as we once lived (in our sinful past lifestyle, Romans 6:11,12).

So, the washing of Acts 22:16 can – and we believe should - be viewed as the cleansing of our ways, the removal of past vices, and the demonstration of a new lifestyle no longer dominated by obvious sin. In a land like the Philippines where the teaching of Ephesians 2:8,9 is so effective against the error of a reliance on good works for salvation, it's sometimes found to be helpful to observe that baptism as a rite or ordinance, is a 'good work' which we do in obedience to the Lord's command and, as such, it cannot bring salvation from sin's penalty. Space forbids, sadly, from expounding the overwhelming biblical case for salvation by faith alone, upon repentance. We'll leave it for you to satisfy yourself that this is the undeniable mainline teaching of the New Testament, beginning with such texts as John 1:12; 3:16; 5:24 etc.

By the way, I'll never forget the sequel to the 2003 seminar we mentioned by way of our opening remarks. As the answers given above were publicly shared, the debaters fell silent and loud 'Amens' punctuated the air in praise of God who'd confirmed his Word!

ABOUT THE AUTHOR

Born and educated in Scotland, Brian worked as a government scientist until God called him into full-time Christian ministry on behalf of the Churches of God (www.churchesofgod.info). His voice has been heard on Search For Truth radio broadcasts for over 30 years (visit www.searchfortruth.podbean.com) during which time he has been an itinerant Bible teacher throughout the UK. His evangelical and missionary work outside the UK is primarily in Belgium, The Philippines and South East Central Africa. He is married to Rosemary, with a son and daughter.

MORE BOOKS BY BRIAN JOHNSTON

MINDFULNESS THAT JESUS ENDORSES

Mindfulness is the trendy meditation offshoot recently endorsed by everyone from National Health Service departments in the UK to Oprah Winfrey in the US. In view of its possible Buddhist origins and the danger of becoming self-absorbed, is there a such a thing as a Biblical Mindfulness that Jesus could endorse? That's the question that Brian answers as he re-introduces us to the transforming power of biblical meditation which, instead of emptying the mind, fills it with a sense of the presence and immediacy of God, and His relevance to what we're experiencing at any moment.

MINOR PROPHETS? MAJOR ISSUES!

The so-called "Minor Prophets" of the Old Testament, such as Nahum, Micah and Malachi, are often overlooked because of their brevity and also because they might seem irrelevant to Christians of today. Brian shows how inaccurate this perception is by pointing out that each prophet not only had vital things to say to the peoples of that era, but they also raise very major issues that are absolutely relevant to believers today. Such issues include: injustice, suffering, unfaithfulness, abandonment, corruption, compassion, arrogance and wrong priorities.

IF ATHEISM IS TRUE...: THE FUTILE FAITH AND HOPELESS HYPOTHESES OF DAWKINS AND CO.

A former nuclear scientist turned missionary, Brian draws together some of his previously published writings on apologetics to produce a concerted offensive against what the apostle Paul would surely describe as the 'indefensible' arguments of the so-called 'New Atheists'. The short chapters in Brian's conversational style serve as an ideal entry-level primer for anyone wanting to get to grips with one of the most important of today's debates.

HEALTHY CHURCHES: GOD'S BIBLE BLUEPRINT FOR GROWTH

As Brian notes in the opening chapters of this book, many churches in the Western world seem to be declining in numbers and spiritual vitality. He explores some of the root causes and also how this trend could be reversed. The good news, as Brian reminds us, is that God gives us the growth blueprint in His Word through a number of key Bible words, such as sowing, reaping, planting, watering, cultivating, building and edifying. Find out the importance of each step in the process and get inspired to go for growth with, in and through, God!

TAKE YOUR MARK'S GOSPEL!

As Brian explains, Mark's Gospel answers the two most important questions that can engage the human mind - who is Jesus is and why did he die? That makes it essential reading for us all - and this accessible commentary unpacks all the key elements as well as providing study questions after each chapter for individual or group study.

ONCE SAVED, ALWAYS SAVED? THE REALITY OF ETERNAL SECURITY

The issue of whether a "born-again" Christian can lose their salvation is an absolutely critical one and has been a controversial topic amongst Christians for centuries. Brian provides a number of faith lessons which include insightful illustrations and Biblical references that all Christians can use to reassure themselves that there is no basis in the Bible for the so-called "Falling Away Doctrine". "For by grace are you saved, through faith."

GET REAL: LIVING EVERY DAY AS AN AUTHENTIC FOLLOWER OF CHRIST

Do you ever feel like you're just playing at being a Christian? Perhaps you even feel a bit of a fake or even a hypocrite - but you don't know what to change or how to change it. Here is some helpful, practical and scriptural guidance on Bible study, personal and collective prayer, worship, church life and family life, with the goal of us becoming authentic, credible disciples who live with real integrity!

ABOUT THE PUBLISHER

Hayes Press (www.hayespress.org) is a registered charity in the United Kingdom, whose primary mission is to disseminate the Word of God, mainly through literature. It is one of the largest distributors of gospel tracts and leaflets in the United Kingdom, with over 100 titles and many thousands dispatched annually. In addition to paperbacks and eBooks, Hayes Press also publishes Plus Eagles' Wings, a fun and educational Bible magazine for children, and Golden Bells, a popular daily Bible reading calendar in wall or desk formats.

If you would like to contact Hayes Press, there are a number of ways you can do so:

By mail: c/o The Barn, Flaxlands, Royal Wootton Bassett, Wiltshire, UK SN4 8DY

By phone: 01793 850598

By eMail: info@hayespress.org

via Facebook: www.facebook.com/hayespress.org

www.ingramcontent.com/pod-product-compliance
Lightning Source LLC
Chambersburg PA
CBHW071819020426
42331CB00007B/1553